Terms like 'digital', 'user-centric' and 'design thinking' are as ubiquitous as they are misunderstood. They are used frequently in the business and innovation spheres, with little thought to what the practices actually entail—or how to achieve the outcomes for clients and customers that they promise. This book provides excellent examples and case studies demonstrating what works, and the way to apply this to your future endeavours. It goes back to basics so that practitioners have an easily digestible guide to truly enacting the age-old adage, putting the customer first.

—**Jade Demnar**, Change Management Consultant, Accenture

The explosion of digital channels and the proliferation of customer data points has created opportunity and challenge in equal measure for many marketers and business leaders. The holy trinity of relevance (what, why, when) has been exponentially complicated by the addition of many 'hows' (channels) and the need for hyper-personalisation at scale. In all of this complexity the primary goal of the marketer often gets left behind. This book provides an excellent reminder that engagement without emotional response is pointless; that as marketers and business leaders we need to constantly remind ourselves that it's our customer's emotions that drive response triggers that result in revenue, affinity, loyalty and amplification. In this increasingly complex world this book illustrates perfectly that we must not tempted by shiny objects and channel trends and stay focused on designing engagement programmes with the customer at the centre.

—**Lee Hawksley**, Senior Vice President, APAC, Salesforce.com

For companies seeking a winning strategy in the digital age, Wrigley and Straker lay out a masterful plan and business case to move beyond customer design to a responsive experience that understands and adapts to customer emotion to create a meaningful connection with brands.

—**Trent Lund**, Head of Innovation and Ventures, PwC

Wrigley and Straker provide a compelling framing of customers' ever-growing demands and complexities provoked through the rise of technology and the compounded impact for businesses needing to re-imagine their products, services and business models to remain relevant. Affected beautifully balances theory, application and case studies to demonstrate a new approach to business innovation.

—**Sophie Tobin**, Strategic Design Director,
BCG Digital Ventures

affected

affected

emotionally engaging customers in the digital age

CARA WRIGLEY & KARLA STRAKER

WILEY

First published in 2018 by John Wiley & Sons Australia, Ltd
42 McDougall St, Milton Qld 4064
Office also in Melbourne

Typeset in 11/13.5pt Adobe Caslon Pro

 A catalogue record for this
book is available from the
National Library of Australia

Cover design by Wrigley & Straker

Cover image © Cj Hendry

Illustrations: Dr Erez Nusem

Printed in Singapore by C.O.S. Printers Pte Ltd

10 9 8 7 6 5 4 3 2 1

Disclaimer
The material in this publication is of the nature of general comment only, and does not represent professional advice. It is not intended to provide specific guidance for particular circumstances and it should not be relied on as the basis for any decision to take action or not take action on any matter which it covers. Readers should obtain professional advice where appropriate, before making any such decision. To the maximum extent permitted by law, the authors and publisher disclaim all responsibility and liability to any person, arising directly or indirectly from any person taking or not taking action based on the information in this publication.

Contents

Foreword

Back in 2005 when I was Head of Marketing Research and Strategy at Philips, we worked on developing products that made sense to people. That is how the Philips slogan 'Sense and Simplicity' came about. Now the slogan is 'Innovation and You'. Innovation is geared towards addressing the emotional needs of users and buyers of products and services. This book presents an innovative and well-researched approach to designing emotional channel engagements and provides a practical path from design innovation 'wow' to design innovation 'how'.

The authors make the point that most companies do not know how to select the right types of channels to reach their audiences. They do not operate well strategically. More particularly, most companies do not really understand at a deeper level the motivations of the users and buyers of their products and are therefore incapable of creating meaningful engagements and loyalty in the new landscape. The authors propose the Digital Affect Framework and offer a typology of digital channels to better equip companies to emotionally engage their customers.

It is often difficult to write a book about such a fast-moving subject. However, Wrigley and Straker provide a practical new approach to design innovation. Their Digital Affect Framework enables customers' latent needs to be addressed through the use of design thinking. All managers who run firms, as well as those responsible for strategic communications that want to compete on value rather than marketing, should familiarise themselves with this approach. This book sets out to accelerate this effort through the Digital Affect Framework, detailed case studies and the key lessons learnt from them, providing and encouraging collaboration for this growing field in design.

Professor Cees de Bont
Dean of the School of Design
The Hong Kong Polytechnic University

About the authors

Associate Professor Cara Wrigley and Dr Karla Straker both reside in the Design Lab—an interdisciplinary research group within the School of Architecture, Design and Planning at The University of Sydney, Australia. They are traditionally trained industrial designers who actively research the value of design in business—specifically through business model strategies that lead to emotive customer engagements.

Prior to their current appointment they spanned faculty appointments in Design, Business, Engineering and Information Technology—emerging in a newly formed discipline, the nexus of design and innovation. Building on solid practical industry experience and combining this with scholarly understanding of emotional design, they have developed a unique insight into innovation in both industry and academia. Through copious industry projects, their work has crossed many disciplinary boundaries and appears in a wide range of high-quality research publications.

Preface

This book was built on friendship — a friendship that started more than a decade ago in a classroom. From our beginnings as the keen, green lecturer and the dedicated student, we have worked together ever since — today as colleagues. Nicknaming ourselves 'Team Foxtail', we were at times forced to downplay our hybrid research to not upset the product-centric discipline in which we once resided.

The nickname comes from British philosopher Isaiah Berlin's parable of the Hedgehog and the Fox. Inspired by Greek poet Archilochus's statement that 'the Fox knows many things, but the Hedgehog knows one big thing.' Berlin stated that people fall into two categories: Hedgehogs, who view the world through a single defining idea, and Foxes, who draw upon wide experiences, and for whom the world is not black and white. The strength of the Hedgehog is his focus on a singular, central vision; the strength of the Fox is his flexibility and openness to complexity. The Hedgehog never wavers or doubts; the Fox is more cautious and more pragmatic.

This concept is a great way to illustrate the problems in business today, where *what* leaders think matters far less than *how* they think. Hedgehogs stay focused and disciplined, and there is no doubt that in the past this has led to success in business. However, Hedgehogs' tendency to ignore what is going on around them can mean that any long-term advantage crumbles. We need more Foxes to lead organisations. Complex thinkers can see game changers in the marketplace that have the power to wipe out competitors overnight. To succeed in this disruptive world, businesses cannot afford to be parochial.

Our salvation, the Fox approach, lies with engaging customers on an emotional level to carefully craft digital relationships online—creating digital *affect*. Affect is the consumer's psychological response to the design and message of a product, service or system (and, more specifically in this book, digital channel). Design is now considered essential to creating and capturing new value through better understanding customers and their emotional needs. Engaging interactions via digital technology earn a customer's trust and emotional investment. However, little is known about emotional design in the impersonal, virtual world in which we now live.

This book was motivated by the constant shift in technology trends, customer demands and increasing global competition that require companies to rethink ways to gain a sustainable competitive advantage. It responds to the increasing need to understand how technology can be used to engage with customers, and takes advantage of the exponential growth of data availability and growing capacity of digital technology to inform and direct strategic decisions. This book addresses the changing cultural, emotional and personal landscape that affects each of us within the business strategy context.

The book is organised into three parts: part I is about the customer, part II is about the company and part III is about the strategy that joins them. Chapter 1 introduces the state of flux businesses are in today and explains the what, why and how of affect from a customer perspective. Chapter 2 details the theories, concepts and importance of understanding emotions and customer relationships. Chapter 3 explains what a digital stimulus is, categorising them into typologies and touchpoints, explaining the complexity of multichannel design and the importance of digital channel consistency. Chapter 4 provides insight into how businesses can compete in a digital world. The final part of this book brings customer and company together, detailing the successful implementation of designing (chapter 5) and managing (chapter 6) an emotional strategy.

There are also three detailed empirical case studies (about the artist Cj Hendry, British brand Burberry and Brisbane Airport) that can be read at any time. As few readers attack a book from cover to cover in one sitting (unless you are perhaps stuck on a plane for a long-haul flight), we have designed the book to be read one chapter at a time.

Throughout these chapters, a variety of examples are used to illustrate success stories but also to highlight mistakes made along the way, and we share ways to overcome them using the perspectives of the Fox and the Hedgehog.

While there is considerable interest in digital channels, there is a limited understanding of their strategic use when engaging with customers. This book, based on more than a decade of research, industry projects and academic articles on this topic, provides a process that will allow your company to sense, learn, respond and adapt your position within an evolving environment — becoming affected.

Despite nearly 150 years of research on emotion, there is still much to learn and in the age of digital disruption, Foxes don't quit!

PART I

Affecting customers

CHAPTER 1

Introducing affect: Creating enduring engagements

Affect (verb): to touch the feelings of; to move emotionally.

It is said that Darwin was the first to research emotions, in his book *The Expression of the Emotions in Man and Animals.* That was nearly 150 years ago. Yet even with over a century of investigation since then, many things still remain unexplained.

Martin Lindstrom's research on cigarette warning labels is a great example to illustrate the complexity of emotions and their effect on behaviour. Participants in the research would report that they were smoking less due to the warnings on cigarette labels (see figure 1.1, overleaf); however, an MRI scan revealed that the centre of the brain associated with desire was stimulated when participants viewed the labels. Surprisingly, the cigarette warnings were creating a *greater* desire to smoke.

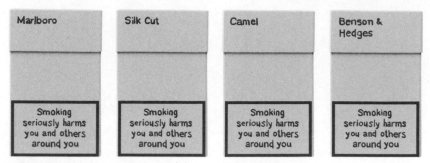

Figure 1.1: plain packaging = more smoking?

This simple example illustrates the complexity of emotions and highlights that our unconscious mind is always active. It shows that our emotions can lead us to behaviours that we may not be able to rationalise. This example also encapsulates the three areas explored in this book:

1. affect (how our brain processes and rationalises emotions)

2. the design of a product, system or environment (the plain packaging and the marketing of the cigarettes)

3. the intended or resultant behaviour (continued smoking).

The complexity of emotions becomes increasingly relevant as our world is forever changing and technology insinuates itself into all aspects of our daily lives. The increased use and interconnectedness of technology has redefined all aspects of modern life. In a news article titled 'Still living in the moment', an elderly woman was photographed at a movie premiere for being the only one NOT taking a photo of Johnny Depp (as shown in figure 1.2). The fact that this was a 'newsworthy' event illustrates the extent to which technology has become an expected part of life; by simply *not* using it, you become the odd one out.

Not only has technology integrated itself into our lives, but it has also disrupted the traditional model of communication for companies. Conventional one-way, company-dominated communication is now a two-way street, creating a power shift between businesses and customers, leaving the customer largely in control.

Figure 1.2: making headlines by still living in the moment

This distribution of power, and the ever-changing field of digital communication, has left companies desperate to understand how best to integrate technology into their business practice. Yet existing commentary overlooks the emotional impact of the daily use of technology.

There is no doubt that technology is affecting the way we communicate, learn, and purchase items, but it is also playing a vital role in influencing our emotions and experiences. Understanding the extent to which interactions through technology can and should influence company strategy is crucial. In the rush to avoid being 'left behind' or the odd one out, many businesses, to their detriment, implement technology with little or no strategic plan at all.

DESIGN THINKING

In recent years, design methods have been recognised as a way to implement customer-centric innovation. In particular, 'design thinking'—seen as a theory for solving complex problems—is increasingly considered the way to develop innovation processes within organisations globally. Tim Brown, one of the creators of the popular press term, explains design thinking as 'a methodology that imbues the full spectrum of innovation activities with a human-centered design ethos'.

Design thinking involves stakeholders throughout all stages of the process, and encompasses the areas of business, people and technology (see figure 1.3). In a commercial world where customers have so many options it's easy to see why this type of thinking has gained so much traction.

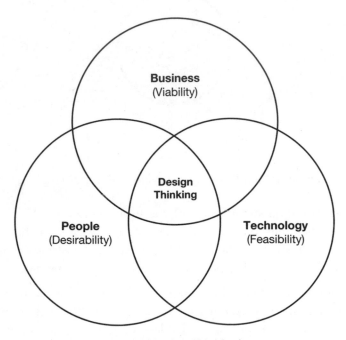

Figure 1.3: at the intersection (design thinking)

Source: Brown, 2006.

Customer empathy is a sizable component of the design thinking process, but the role that emotions play within this is not yet well understood. In Dan Hill's book *Emotionomics* he explains that by focusing on customers' unarticulated aspirations, companies can become better informed and nimbler.

However, to better understand how emotions can be used to design digital engagements, we need to explore virtual relationships in depth, understanding the ways we process information and perform tasks, and how this influences our motivations, arouses certain feelings and affects our behaviours.

Therefore, the focus of this book is at the intersection of emotion (people), strategy (business) and digital channels (technology): to understand how to emotionally engage customers in the digital age (see figure 1.4).

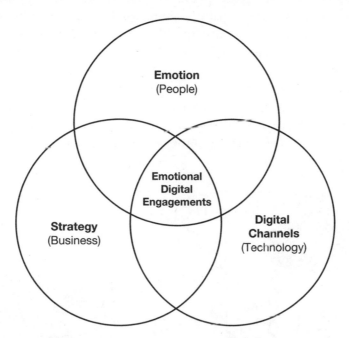

Figure 1.4: at the intersection (emotional digital engagements)

AFFECT AND COMPANIES

Digital innovation has created an entirely new class of competition for businesses. The explosion of available data and the growing capabilities of technology have provided companies with valuable information when making strategic decisions. As a result, technology has moved beyond functional applications, towards a more strategic role.

The challenge for companies is to keep up with these changes and develop new theories, models and methods to learn, respond, and adapt their position in such competitive environments. An example of this is Kodak's failure to anticipate how social technologies (such as Instagram) connect people, facilitate the sharing of visual experiences and morph the meaning of photography.

Kodak's missed moment

Kodak held a strong market position for many years until the late 1990s, when they began to struggle financially as a result of their slowness in transitioning to digital photography. It is therefore surprising to learn that Kodak actually developed the first digital camera in 1975, but did not release it as they feared it would threaten their current business model built on selling film for their cameras. The following years saw digital cameras became commodities. Kodak's slow reaction and their fear of product development led them to fall behind the competition throughout the 2000s. They also failed to realise that online photo sharing *was* the new business, not just a way to expand the printing business. People went from printing pictures to sharing them online (see figure 1.5).

Figure 1.5: Kodak to Instagram

Kodak failed to see the disruption of technology but, more importantly, they missed how people would use photos. They failed to anticipate how:

- such a technology might connect people
- photography might morph from a professional and recreational activity into a social currency
- the camera might become integrated into a new way of life.

These failures sent Kodak into bankruptcy in 2012. If only Kodak had kept true to their original value offering: 'share memories, share life'.

Kodak and others (as listed in figure 1.6) are examples of companies that have been disrupted by digital platforms that gave them little opportunity to respond before it was too late—the competitor was already on the global market and had the advantage of scalability.

If businesses don't stay on top of how customers are feeling and why they emotionally value or don't value their product or service, they leave themselves vulnerable to disruption, as these three (Hedgehog-mentality) businesses did.

Hedgehog		Fox
Kodak	⟶	Instagram
Cabcharge	⟶	Uber
Accor Hotels	⟶	Airbnb

Figure 1.6: overnight disruptors

Second that emotion

Emotions are probably not the first thing to come to mind when thinking about business strategy. Most established companies are experts on the operational and economical aspects that make up their competitive market position. Having strong manufacturing and production knowledge, as well as promotional and advertising competencies, they are usually guided by traditional marketing research methods. They try to understand their customers with surveys, focus groups and questionnaires asking customers what they want. But while this approach lets customers express their preferences for incremental elements in existing products and services (such as choosing one colour over another) they struggle to express their latent needs and desires, let alone the emotions driving these preferences.

Design has become a way to uncover the emotional meaning of products and services through understanding customers better. By using design methods, businesses can engage with their customers on a deeper level to understand not *what* they want but *why* they want it, knowledge that can inform their overall strategy and approach to communication.

Designers are aware of the importance of creating strong emotional experiences intertwined with tangible products, as emotions influence the success of product update. However, not all interactions include tangible products. Companies that provide services rather than tangible products also face the challenge of acquiring insight into customers' needs.

In order to survive, companies must create deeper connections with their customers beyond just product-centred interactions.

Some believe that design has become *the* differentiator for businesses looking to innovate. Design is a great way to approach complex problems systematically, as a designer's mindset equips them to see problems as opportunities for the invention of new alternatives. Designers can also translate insights from diverse stakeholders into a form that is useful within design projects. Drawing on their creative, intellectual and visualisation skills to translate abstract concepts into concrete ideas.

The overall aim of a design approach is to gain a deeper understanding of customers, by knowing what they value rather than being informed only by their user requirements. This approach requires knowledge which spans the fields of design, technology and people (see figure 1.3.)

Much has been written about the ability of design to increase productivity, product performance and engagement with customers, but comparatively little focus has been given to design thinking's influence on the holistic understanding of the customer's emotional experience. There has been much discussion surrounding the role of the customer in driving innovation efforts, but not the process for uncovering, comprehending and understanding customers' unspoken latent needs. This is due to the fact that such insights are almost always unspoken, often unconscious and laced with multifaceted needs and desires, making them difficult to infuse into a company-wide strategy.

DEFINING AFFECT

Most people associate emotions with words such as happy, sad, excited or angry; however, in psychology the word 'affect' is commonly used interchangeably with the word 'emotion'. 'Affect' is used to describe the topics of emotions, feelings and moods collectively. The definitions of feelings, emotions and mood that follow were first proposed by Paul Thomas Young in 1961.

Feelings are subjective representations of emotions, private to the individual experiencing them. There are different types of feelings, depending on the way they are triggered, either internal (physical) feelings or external (social) feelings. Feelings evoke emotions. Examples of feelings are to feel *regret, worried, curious, threatened* or *impressed*.

Emotions are brief, but often intense, mental and physiological feeling states. In comparison with moods, emotions are shorter lived, stronger, and more specific forms of affect. Emotions are caused by specific events; we generally only experience them when things are out of the ordinary or unusual, whereas we experience moods in normal, everyday situations. Examples of emotions are *jealously, anger, fear, pride* and *love*.

A **mood** is a long-term affective state and is triggered by a combination of emotions. They generally last for a much longer duration and are usually less intense than emotions. The main difference between emotion and mood is that people are more aware of their mood and therefore can express it more readily. Examples of moods are to be *anxious, irritable, disappointed, mellow* or *stressed*.

Figure 1.7 illustrates these concepts.

Feelings ──── **Evoke** ────▸ **Emotions** ──── **Trigger** ────▸ **Moods**

Figure 1.7: affective states: feelings, emotions and moods

These different affective states are important as they make up a consumer's emotional experience with a company. The process of an emotional experience, whether between people or between people and technology, is complex and involves many differing factors; however, it is the states of affect (emotions, feelings and mood) that has the greatest influence. Understanding customers and their emotional experiences is important for future planning and knowing what is needed to build a strong relationship over time.

Neuroscientist Antonio Damasio explains emotions as changes in both body and brain states in response to different stimuli, illustrating that emotions are more than an internal personal process, but rather made up of three connected components:

1. cognition (what we think)

2. affect (what we feel)

3. behaviour (what we do).

A typical process (as illustrated in figure 1.8) begins with a perception of the stimulus before the engagement, which leads to thoughts and evaluations (cognitive) about a stimulus and triggers a bodily response (affect). According to Damasio, these emotions are crucial in the decision making process and the action (behaviour) that businesses are seeking to influence.

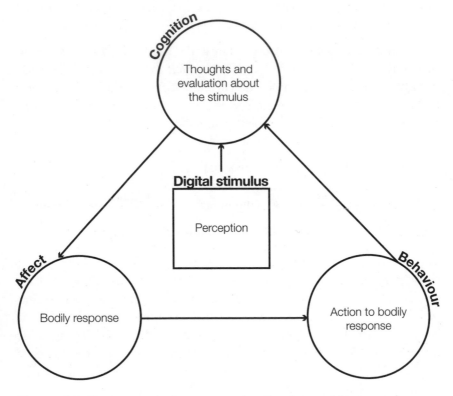

Figure 1.8: the connected components of an internal framework

Remember the example of warning labels on cigarettes from the beginning of this chapter? Let's look at it in the context of the internal process framework in figure 1.9. The smoker's perception of the stimulus (plain packaged cigarettes) is that it reduces the desire to smoke, which leads to a smoker's thinking that smoking is reduced (cognitive); however, unconsciously the bodily response to the stimulus is a desire to smoke (affect), creating the action of smoking (behaviour).

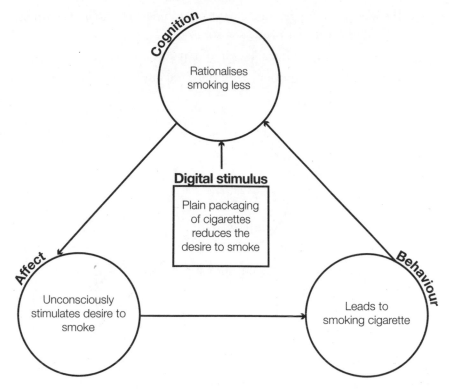

Figure 1.9: the emotional experience of smoking

Our framework for the process of designing digital channel engagements is based on Damasio's theory and the intersection of the fields of business strategy and digital technology. Similar to Damasio's theory, this model (shown in figure 1.10, overleaf) includes the fundamental emotional response to stimulus in a situation, however it focuses on the experience of digital engagement.

It illustrates that cognition (what we think), affect (what we feel), and behaviour (what we do) are related and influence each other. The model starts with an engagement with stimulus from a company (digital), and has three phases:

1. It begins with an existing association of feelings, emotions and moods to the company (cognition).

2. An interaction with the company's digital channel will evoke a feeling, emotion or mood (affect).

3. The interaction triggers and creates an attitude, behaviour or meaning towards the company (behaviour).

This process is a loop, as the experience will either reinforce or alter the original associations (cognition) with the company.

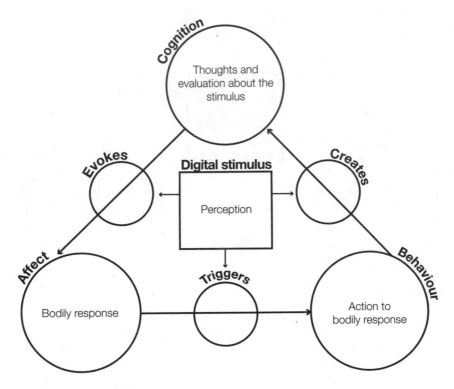

Figure 1.10: the Affect Framework

This process requires a deeper analysis of customers' emotions and their engagements with digital channels than is customary. In this book we provide perspective on how stimulus is processed, responded to, and the outcomes it produces, in the context of customers' digital channel experiences.

This framework (see figure 1.10) is built upon throughout the chapters in this book, to provide details as to how companies can align their company strategy with their customers' needs and desires. Digital channels present an opportunity to design or improve a customer's experience, but this must start with an understanding of affect.

THE AFFECT EFFECT

The digital era has created many exciting opportunities for companies to engage with their customers. No longer are customers simply downloading or searching for static data; instead, they are engaging, uploading and sharing their own content via social networks.

While information technology was traditionally used for functional and operational purposes, it is now a strategic asset. Indeed, these technologies not only provide value to the customer, but also enable companies to gather strategic insights to gain a competitive advantage.

A customer's interaction in a store or website, with employees, or through a long-term loyalty program, can all affect a customer's experience. These encounters between customers and companies are referred to as 'channels'. A channel refers to how a company communicates and reaches its customers to deliver its value proposition. Most companies employ a mix of channels that span the customer journey, including pre, post and during the experience. The vast quantity of channels available to the customer during these phases has increased considerably in the past decade, with the subsequent increase of competition between channels (for example, targeted Facebook and Instagram adverts competing with those on radio and television) making them a progressively important area for companies to innovate.

Traditionally, the focus of channels has been on the functional aspects of a company's distribution system (manufacturers, wholesalers, distributors, retailers) involved in making an offering available to the customer. This perspective has shifted. Now channels are a way to deliver positive customer experiences and create value. However, the integration of technology also led to the expectation that customers are able to engage and communicate with companies at all times. Meaning that companies should choose carefully which digital channels they use, as being active is one of the key requirements of successful digital channel design.

Digital channels allow companies to build relationships with customers and gain information, which should help them to respond better to their customers' needs. This information (referred to as 'customer insights') is a strategic asset, as when used correctly it can give a company a competitive advantage by enhancing the customer experience.

'Digital strategy' is explained as to align a company's business strategy and information technology to gain a competitive advantage.

A digital strategy, still a relatively new area of business management, is the strategic use of information technology within an organisation. There is currently a lack of research concerning how businesses should collect, analyse and implement customer insights gained from digital channels, and companies often lack people with the digital strategy experience required to take full advantage of these insights. When selecting and implementing digital channels, the first thing to understand is how customers use and communicate through them. The opportunity that a successful digital strategy provides is to allow organisations to synchronise business and information technology to gain a competitive advantage.

Many forward-thinking retailers, such as Starbucks, Victoria's Secret and Kate Spade, have achieved successful digital strategies by providing engaging experiences. In this book we define an experience to involve:

- the customer's response to the company (affect)

- elements controlled by the company (service, retail atmosphere, price)

- elements out of the company's control (influence of others, purpose of shopping).

An example of a unique digital engagement is fashion brand Kate Spade, which became aware that their customers' expectations were drastically changing due to digital technology, and aimed to understand their customers better. Kate Spade's goal was to evoke desired emotions that reflect the brand's identity and to match the way they envisioned their customers would like to respond to and interact with a channel.

Kate Spade introduced digital 'window shopping'. Four storefronts scattered throughout Manhattan were painted bright yellow with black-and-white graphic patterns (signature to Kate Spade). The windows were designed to accommodate the 'Kate Spade Saturday Girl': a girl who looks for adventure around every corner. Apparel and accessories were displayed on hangers and hooks inside the windows. These window stores only existed for one month but were open 24 hours a day. Passers-by could use the storefronts to get a preview of merchandise from the new line. Next to the merchandise was a large touchscreen (see figure 1.11) where users browsed sizes and colours, and placed orders for free delivery anywhere in Manhattan within an hour. The purchase process simply required entering a mobile phone number, with a confirmation text sent. A bike messenger delivered the products, and, just like a take-out food order, payment happened upon delivery. In this scenario, the Saturday Girl 'gets what she wants, where she wants it.'

Figure 1.11: Kate Spade's digital window shopping

DIGITAL AFFECT

Designers seek to design experiences that foster positive connections with their users. Although it's not an exact science, this is usually done through understanding users and their pre, during and post interaction with a product, service or company. The design and management of digital channels is an opportunity to strengthen brand recognition and create a loyal customer base. Designers are capable of designing products, services and experiences that embody the brand values of an organisation.

The current problem is the absence of research to guide practitioners on which digital channel to use, how to use it and why. The company and customer are connected via digital channels, but many of the channels that companies engage in only allow one-way communication. Such a decision can lead to a loss of communication opportunities and control of digital channels. As channels play a vital role in the customer experience, they are an opportunity to create and maintain engagement with customers.

This book explores the dynamic relationship between company and customer values, emotions and behaviours within a digital context. The framework (see figure 1.10) starts with an engagement with stimulus from a company (digital). Existing perceptions of the company or brand lead us to have thoughts and evaluations about this stimulus (cognitive), which evokes a bodily response (affect), triggering an action (behaviour), which reinforces or creates new perceptions.

An emotional engagement develops when a customer identifies with the values of a company. The importance of a 'sense of meaning' is heavily explored in the field of design and emotion, as the customer's mindset is a key driver in what companies they choose to engage with. If the customer is repeatedly engaging in the experience, it will have a significant effect on their associations with and perception of the company. One example of this is Meat Pack.

Meat Pack is a shoe retailer in Guatemala celebrated for its edgy, audacious style. The store is renowned for offering unique discounts on limited-edition kicks (shoes), from brands such as Nike, adidas and Reebok. Meat Pack rapidly mustered a cult youth following, emerging as a hero in the 'sneakerhead' subculture.

When they decided to unveil a new promotion, this particular campaign, 'Hijack', distilled their brand values by constantly surprising their customers, offering an innovative, participatory way to earn the discount. 'Hijack', an enhancement for the official Meat Pack mobile app, used GPS tracking technology that recognised when customers entered a competitor's store (see figure 1.12). This would trigger an offer for a discount. The discount started at 99 per cent and with each second that passed, it would be reduced by one per cent. The countdown urged users to hurry towards the nearest Meat Pack store; the faster they reached the store, the bigger the discount. Users had to earn their discount by running.

Figure 1.12: hijacking customers: an app to drive behaviours

This digital engagement 'hijacked' customers away from the competitors, not only through hefty discounts but also through making customers aware of the brand via an active digital presence. 'Hijack' offers a different approach to the traditional discount voucher that aligns with their company values and targeted trendy and edgy customers (cognitive). The experience of using the mobile app undoubtedly is a fun and memorable one (affect), translating to a significant behaviour change (running from a competitor's store).

The longstanding effects on behaviour are documented via the company's additional social media channels such as Facebook and Twitter, which are tasked with promoting the brand through these engaging and positive experiences. That digital campaign was successful, as within the first week more than 600 shoppers were 'hijacked' from the competitors, with one of them receiving an 89 per cent discount. Figure 1.13 (overleaf) shows the Digital Affect Framework that Hijack employed. Gone are the days when a piece of paper stamped with the word 'voucher' is a promise of sales, nor does it hold the interest of, or appeal to, your target audience in a unique way. Weekend offers, discounts and specials are the new norm for most retail outlet brands, especially in the sneaker market, with 'Hijack' completely changing the way discounting and sales have traditionally been done.

One of the main objectives of design is to offer a unique experience to customers in order to improve or produce a positive affect. The design takes the customer beyond products, services, spaces and technology to provide an experience with emotional value. The aim is to establish and enhance customer trust and commitment to influence behaviours, leading to increased sales and performance. This is important because we do not always make informed, rational decisions, but are driven by subjective factors such as emotions. Emotion is the link between experience and subsequent behaviours. We learn to choose products, services or experiences that are instrumental to achieving our desired outcomes, whatever they may be.

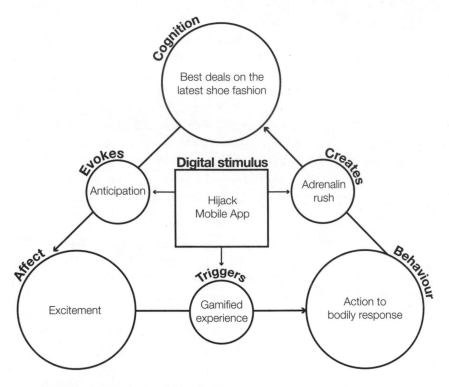

Figure 1.13: Hijack Digital Affect Framework

Marketing research has proven that memorable positive experiences lead to positive behaviours towards a company, and in turn form loyal customers. In addition, a customer's perceptions of the investment made by the company in digital engagements can affect the relationship quality and their willingness to provide and share positive experiences with others.

This chapter has introduced the concept of affect and the Affect Framework. In the chapters to come we will build and expand upon this framework, detailing each component.

CHAPTER 2

Customer drivers: Emotion, affect and the hedonic pursuit

Humans have always sought pleasure. We've gained enjoyment over the years from nature: from bathing in gentle waters, the seduction of sunset, and the refreshment of a cool breeze. We have actively sought pleasure by creating activities and pastimes to stretch our mental and physical capabilities or to express our creativity. Cave dwellers wrestled to test their strength and expressed themselves through painting on the walls of their dwellings. Today, we add another source of pleasure to this list: the products and services with which we surround ourselves.

'Hedonics' is the study of the pursuit of pleasure, and in this book, it's the examination of how an individual actively pursues pleasure by responding to certain objects and experiences. In short, people are passionate about their belongings.

Shopping, as a social activity, is an inherently hedonic pursuit. A need for hedonic design logically follows: design that delivers the sought-after hedonic experience of consumption—a pleasurable product purchase and usage experience.

Shopping has been driven into the digital age (as seen in the Kate Spade example, Figure 1.11, see p17.) Therefore, this chapter explores the concept of hedonics through the digital consumer. The goal? To create digital affect. This chapter will expand your understanding of emotions to explore how products and experiences can create meaning and reflect our values.

EMOTIONS 101

There is a lack of consensus in existing research as to the definition of emotions. In 1960 Paul Ekman classified emotions by having his research participants contort their facial muscles into distinct expressions. From this, six emotions were classified as basic: anger, disgust, happiness, fear, sadness and surprise.

Robert Plutchik confirmed Ekman's biologically-led viewpoint and extended it to become a 'wheel of emotions', proposing a positive or negative footing for eight primary emotions: joy versus sadness; anger versus fear; trust versus distrust; and surprise versus anticipation. In some cases, basic emotions can evolve into more complex (or secondary) emotions. Such complex emotions can result from primary, basic emotions being combined with cultural conditioning. These include envy, jealousy, anxiety, guilt, shame, relief, hope, depression, pride, love, gratitude and compassion. Alternatively, similar to the way primary colours can be combined, primary emotions can mix to form complex emotions.

Emotions are as difficult to define as they are to measure. Studies have had subjects self-report using verbal scales or protocols, and non-verbal instruments such as visual cues and photosets. Emotions have also been gauged by measuring physiological reactions, such as changes in heart rate or pupil dilation, that are associated with emotions.

EMOTIONS AND AFFECT

'Emotion', 'feeling' and 'affect' have many overlapping uses in the social sciences. Companies aim to lead customers to action, hence 'affect' is a more useful principle than 'emotion' as it provides the context for *how* the emotion is gained. As explained in chapter 1, 'affect' is used to describe the topics of emotions, feelings and moods collectively, and is commonly used interchangeably with emotion.

Table 2.1 shows the conditions that arouse certain affective states as synthesised from the work of Pieter Desmet. While a broad emotional spectrum is catalogued in the table, since this book focuses on hedonic emotions (ones in the pursuit of pleasure), these are the ones that are isolated and further discussed. (This is because the majority of organisations wish for their customers to experience only positive emotions during their interaction with the company.)

Table 2.1: conditions that elicit affective states

Eliciting condition	Affective state
Approving of one's own praiseworthy action	Pride
Fearing the worst but yearning for better	Hope
Approving of someone else's praiseworthy action	Admiration
An object calls for possession or usage	Desire
A promise for understanding through exploration or a new action	Stimulation
The realisation of an expected goal	Satisfaction
Liking a desirable or pleasant event	Enjoyment
The realisation of an unexpected goal	Pleasant surprise
Liking an appealing object	Love (liking)
Disapproving of one's own blameworthy action	Shame
Wanting what someone else has	Jealousy
Facing an immediate, concrete, physical danger	Fear
A demeaning offence against me and mine	Anger
Having experienced an irrevocable loss	Sadness
A better goal realisation than expected	Relief
An unwanted lack of stimulation	Boredom
Disapproving of someone else's blameworthy action	Contempt
Revulsion towards something considered offensive or unpleasant	Disgust
A lesser goal realised than hoped for	Disappointment
A lesser goal realised than expected	Dissatisfaction
To hold one's attention pleasantly	Amusement
An unexpected goal obstruction	Unpleasant surprise

Source: Synthesised from Desmet, 2005.

COGNITION, AFFECT AND BEHAVIOUR

Social psychology is based on the ABCs of affect, behaviour and cognition:

Affect	Behaviour	Cognition
(Emotions)	(Interactions)	(Thought)

All three work together to produce the customer experience. The emotions we feel during consumption experiences are glimpses into the unconscious mind of the consumer. The initial experience with a product (stimulus) creates the emotional and symbolic value, i.e. its meaning.

Pleasurable experiences with a stimulus over a period of time will create an emotional attachment. This has many implications for marketing and advertising, as the customer experience is vital in building up brand loyalty and driving repeat business. However, this has become harder and harder to do as customer expectations have increased in the digital age.

One example of a new digital channel designed to provide their customers with a unique store experience is the Australian women's clothing store Sportsgirl. They introduced a 'digital change room' (an interactive mirror) in one of their Melbourne stores. It worked by taking a photo of the customer after they had come out of the change room in their newly tried-on outfit. Using the touch screen display, customers could then share the photo on social media sites for their network to vote on. After receiving feedback from their friends online they could opt to purchase the outfit even after leaving the store, and have it promptly delivered to their door.

In this case Sportsgirl were able to tap into their customers' mindset by following their existing behaviour: either going shopping with friends to get their opinions, or taking selfies inside the change rooms and sending them to friends for approval. With the digital change room they were able to capitalise on both behaviours and leverage their online brand presence.

Another example of behaviour shifts was in 2014 during the World Cup. Pepsi launched a campaign where customers who purchased their special edition cans could play a football game on their smartphone by scanning the code on the can. Augmented reality technology was used to create the impression of firing cans at a virtual goalpost 'on' the Pepsi can or bottle, playing against the world's top five World Cup players. Over 60 000 hours were played on their game, with Pepsi brand placement being front and centre at all times. This had the additional benefit of providing Pepsi with valuable customer data in real time, such as how many users were interacting with it, how many times they did so, the lengths of the interaction and their location. Figure 2.1 shows the Digital Affect experience of this Pepsi campaign. When someone first learns about the campaign, they could see it as a creative way to join the world cup experience. This then evokes a sense of competition and enjoyment through the gamified experience, and the behavioural impact of this experience is through the hours spent on the mobile app, and in sharing this experience with others.

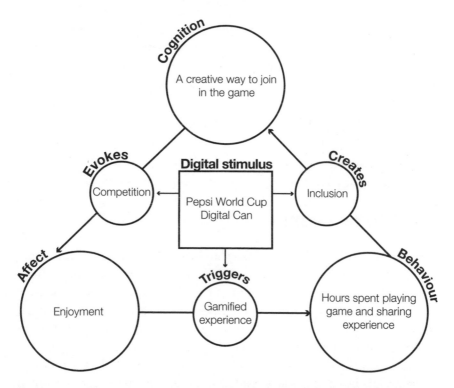

Figure 2.1: Pepsi's World Cup campaign Digital Affect Framework

They gamified the experience of drinking a fizzy cola and, more importantly, sold out of all the limited-edition cans. (They're now a collector's item.) This took sports sponsorship to a whole new level, as gamifying the experience led customers to feel a part of the World Cup in a way that a soft drink brand had never done before. This approach is similar to that of Meat Pack, discussed in chapter 1.

This example can be seen as one of a set of interactions (human to human, user to product, customer to company) that will evoke an affective response, starting with feelings, which evoke emotions that over time will create a mood. The affective response to the interaction will inform the customer's experience, which can change their attitude, behaviour and associated meaning towards the initial interaction. It is believed that this process will need to happen more than once and produce a consistent affective state through the experience in order to change behaviour and influence attitude and meaning.

Damasio's theories (discussed in chapter 1 and illustrated in figure 1.10, see p14) illustrate that cognition (what we think), emotion (what we feel) and behaviour (what we do) are related and influence each other. A customer's expectations, evaluations and perceptions of an experience trigger an emotion, resulting in a behavioural response or output.

Emotion envelops design. Fundamentally, all the choices and judgements we make in life are based on either how we feel, or how we think we will feel. The field of neuroscience has proven that without an emotional response, we would find it difficult to make the simplest of decisions, such as deciding between tea or coffee in the morning.

THE LIFE OF PRODUCTS

The interaction between consumers and products elicits an emotional response. Affect is a part of the consumer's response to the sensory attributes or design message of a product. Consumers may experience a variety of emotions, potentially contradictory, in response to a product. These emotions may include intrigue, disappointment, satisfaction or amusement. However, they typically can be confined to a limited selection of possible emotions and, as they are directed at a product, can generally be categorised as on the less extreme end of the emotional scale.

The following are examples of such elicited product emotions from Cara's history. (Karla is too young to remember analog phones and too sensible to have such ridiculous hedonic purchases plague her past.)

Juicy Salif

Juicy Salif (the spaceship-looking citrus-juicer) designed by Philippe Starck (see figure 2.2) is a truly iconic design object of the past century.

Figure 2.2: Juicy Salif — Philippe Starck

In my days as an industrial design student, many of my peers had this Alessi-made product marked as number one on their Christmas wish list. This juicer was a must-have for all envious design students who worshipped the form and function debate Starck entertained in his designs. This juicer took pride of place on coffee tables, bathroom shelves, and even on some bedside mantels in crowded student share houses—everywhere except the kitchen drawer (where most juicers are kept). I loved it! It represents all things design—good design and affective design (see figure 2.3).

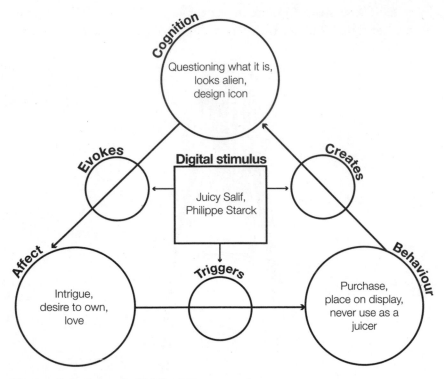

Figure 2.3: Juicy Salif Affect Framework

Smart Roadster

Fast-forward to five years later. Upon graduating from design school, I purchased my first car: the Mercedes-owned Smart Roadster. Nicknamed 'Smartie', she was gold and black with Lamborghini doors (that opened upwards—see figure 2.4).

Figure 2.4: Smart Roadster — Mercedes-Benz

To the young designer I was at the time, it drove like a Lotus. Now, upon reflection, I realise it was more like a go-kart. I took out a huge loan to buy that car, paying the exact figure the dealer had advertised (so young and naive)—but I loved that car like it was a member of the family, as ridiculous as that sounds. It had very little space and I couldn't get much more than two bags of groceries in the front boot. It was so low to the ground you felt like your backside was barely hovering above the road. Sporting a 60-kilowatt motorbike engine, it might not have been the safest choice of car for the rough Australian roads. Regardless of all its impracticalities, it was loved!

In the end, it had to be sold back to Mercedes in order to finance the purchase of a house. It was a sensible financial decision at the time. When I walked away from the dealership that day, I felt the same emotional distress as if I were saying a final goodbye to the family dog at the veterinary clinic. It truly felt like a missing limb. Figure 2.5 (overleaf) illustrates the Affect Framework for the Smart Roadster.

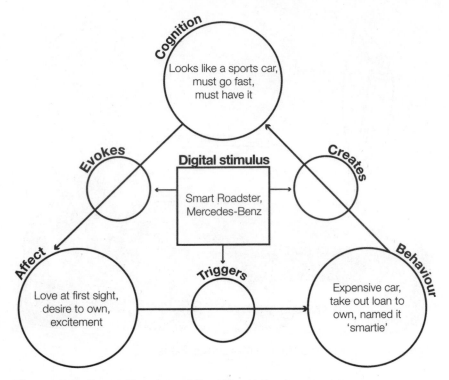

Figure 2.5: Smart Roadster Affect Framework

Lipstick phone

Fast-forward another few years to my days as a postgraduate student—a time well before the smartphone. Nokia were the biggest player in town. Their point of differentiation was their ever-changing physical designs, as well as the game Snake. While most mobile phones were flip-oriented or brick-like, the one I purchased was dubbed the 'lipstick phone'—for its unusual shape and mirror façade (see figure 2.6).

The mixed textures of leather, plastic, mirror and decorative decals was such an intriguing design. It had a matching lanyard so it could be worn around the neck like a piece of jewellery. In order to type a text message, you had to scroll through the alphabet using the circular dial until you found the letter or number you required and then press the centre button to select. You can imagine how time-consuming it was to send a text message. As a result, calls were made instead, resulting in many painfully large phone bills every month. Regardless—this phone was also loved (see figure 2.7).

Figure 2.6: Nokia 'lipstick' phone

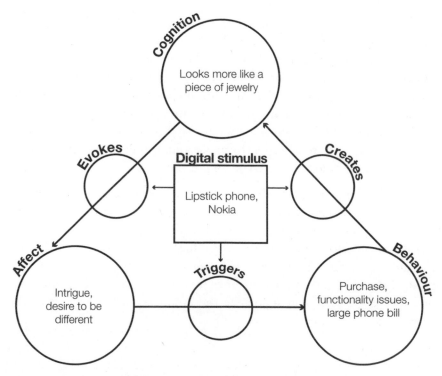

Figure 2.7: Nokia 'lipstick' phone Affect Framework

DESIGNING FOR EMOTION

Designers need to understand emotions and the lengths to which people will go in order to pursue a hedonic experience. This knowledge should inform their design decisions, resulting in better, more enjoyable products, services and systems.

Back in the 1990s we realised that designing for implicit and explicit product qualities, such as form and function, was no longer enough. We needed to now design for the holistic interaction between consumer and company over time. Today, not only does the design approach have to create positive experiences before, during and after product interaction, an organisation also needs to elicit the same emotional experience across all products, services and channels (intended and unintended).

Both our behaviour and cognition—at an individual level and also in social surroundings—influence affect. Emotional affect can change how we process thoughts by changing how we perceive and interpret the world around us.

The nature of the circumstance (for example stressful/dangerous or trivial/relaxed) has an impact on how we process thought. In the majority of cases, cognitive thought follows the same path as affect. When deciding whether or not to purchase a product or service in a relaxed situation, we will draw from our unconscious affective responses to make a decision. Compare this to the purchase of a large investment in the stock market (for most a stressful situation): conscious appraisal and knowledge are relied upon to make a judgement and unconscious affective cues should be ignored or suppressed.

Take this concept into the design field. It is the designer's role to cater to sought-out hedonic experiences by communicating to the consumer through the physicality of their design. Introducing 'product rhetoric', the process of product communication. Product rhetoric is communicating the message from the designer (source) through the medium of the product (transmitter) to the consumer (receiver), thus enabling them to understand, perceive and appreciate the product and the value it holds (as seen in figure 2.8).

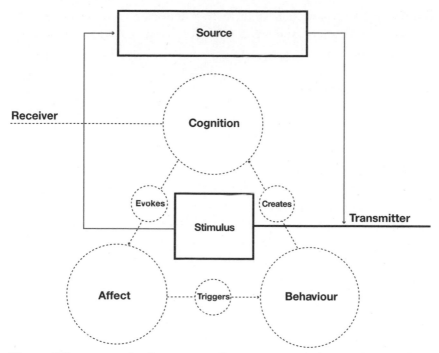

Figure 2.8: communication connection: source, receiver and transmitter

Shannon's model of communication

Claude Shannon's basic model of communication is a useful way to examine the dialogue between designer and consumer. The designer (or anyone involved with creating the product or message) is the source of the communication, transmitting their message via the product they design; thus, the product becomes the transmitter of the design intent. The environment within which the consumer and product interact becomes the medium by which the message is transferred from source to receiver. The consumer appraises the product using sensory information; thus, the consumer's sensory perception can be considered to be the receiver of the design message, much like a radio receives radio waves that are then converted into sound. Continuing the analogy, the interpretation of radio waves to produce sound can be likened to the consumer's ability to interpret sensory information, to process and act in response to the product. Much like the production of sound, the consumer's response can be considered the 'destination' of Shannon's communication model.

Studies into consumer behaviour further delineate such a response into 'cognition' and 'affect' and a corresponding, and outwardly observable, 'behaviour' or action.

Product experiences

A connection can be created with the consumer when products elicit, communicate and share emotions. Designers elicit emotions through the manipulation of the sensory qualities of a product. However, emotional satisfaction can only be achieved if the product collaborates with the user in a positive experience. Rather than singling out emotion as an object of attention and working to explicitly trigger it, it is more fruitful to recognise emotion as a multilayered, emergent aspect of experience. Therefore, experience, where the subject and object meet and merge, becomes a key issue in designing emotionally meaningful stimuli.

Emotions are a biologically and experientially determined process and, although rough correspondence can be made between a class of emotion inducer and the resulting emotion, particular emotional responses vary from person to person. An individual's stage of development, knowledge, environment and culture are just some of the influencing factors that alter the expression of emotions and their meaning to the individual.

A variety of needs are fulfilled by consumer products, including aspirations and cultural, social and emotional needs. The relationship between a product and its consumer has created a great amount of interest in various product innovation and marketing fields; every object is significant in its own way to each individual through different memories and experiences. Thus, a designer must develop their designs to meet and empathise with the specific user group targeted by the product.

In general, a designer works in a space that is constrained by a number of outside variables such as cost, time to market, brand identity or style, internal organisational communication issues, resources and so on. All these influences moderate the effectiveness of the consequent design in transmitting its intended message. For example, a designer given a quick time frame to design for an emergent niche may be required to spend less time on the product design, with more time spent on researching the market. So the appearance of the product may not be as appealing to its consumers as anticipated. Similarly, budget limitations may reduce the achievable quality and finish of the materials used.

The individual differences between consumers result not only in variations in the preferences they express, but also in the importance of those preferences. For example, some people place more value on the appearance of products than others.

A consumer's response is also heavily moderated by cultural influences, which contribute to how a design is interpreted and to what extent it is accepted by the consumer. This can become even more complicated if the designer and consumer are from different cultures.

A consumer's personal situation at the time of viewing a product also has the potential to influence their response. For example, their financial situation may dictate the price range of products they will consider and whether a product may or may not be purchased.

Cognitive appraisals

Once knowledge is acquired about the product, we rely on these cognitive appraisals to make further decisions. For example, once the Juicy Salif was decided upon (drawn from affective reasoning), the decision of whether to purchase the gold-plated version was consciously deciphered (gold plating reacts with the acidity in the juice if you were actually going to use it). These cognitive appraisals also take into consideration how we would navigate the task the product is designed to carry out. Now, not all decisions and interactions are as simple and as quickly carried out as this example. The impact of cognitive appraisals is much more obvious when the information is ambiguous (rather than strongly positive or negative) — the affect is reduced.

Affective states raise or lower our motivation by fluctuating the amount of physiological stimulation or angst, influencing cognition. This is due to the fact that we can easily recall events and experiences that occurred when we were in a similar state of arousal. Such nostalgia allows consumers to reflect on their direct experience with an object, and the meaning is unique to each individual.

Changing the meaning of products

The meaning of a product is powerful. Following are two examples of how the meaning of a product can change, for the better or worse.

Nintendo Wii

This last decade, the 'PlayStation vs Xbox' console rivalry has consumed the marketplace of the gaming world. With both jostling for control of the sector, competition was fierce and cutthroat. They competed for the most part on high-end, realistic graphics and sound, creating addictive gaming environments. This kind of investment from Microsoft and Sony did not come cheap, and as a result research and development budgets ran high and were constantly expanding in the race to beat each other in technology advancement. Their target customer was the addictive gamer, usually male, aged between 18 and 35, who would spend on average 40 hours a week playing along with people online.

Until a third competitor joined the ranks: the Nintendo Wii. It was the simplistic underdog of the gaming sector. Why? Because instead of joining their competitors and jamming their consoles with the most high-powered tech they could find in an effort to appeal to serious gamers, Nintendo developed the Wii—a lovable, low-cost, gesture-controlled console that innovated by targeting a broader demographic, from 8 to 80. Its competitors were family trips to the cinema or the family board game night. Unconventional? Maybe. But by looking outside the gaming world at different types of competitors, such as the cinema, and changing the meaning of the product, it successfully disrupted the marketplace.

Nintendo's turnaround began when they looked to address two troubling trends: their targeted consumer began to limit their gaming time to focus on their family and careers; and as technology became more advanced producing games become more expensive, with these costs being passed on to the consumer.

The technology was more than a decade old, the graphics were simple and, while their competitors lost money with every console they made, hoping to make it back with the high-profit margins on their games, the Wii was designed to be immediately profitable. The meaning for the product went from addictive gaming to inclusive gaming. Nintendo realised that if they changed their product and what a video game meant to a different market, they would change the behaviour of those using it.

'Gaming' was no longer just a solo online activity held in dark basements with large TV screens and headsets; it was instead a Friday night in with the family playing Wii tennis (see figure 2.9).

Figure 2.9: changing the meaning of gaming: Sony vs Nintendo

Driven away from cars

Another example of an obvious shift in meaning in recent years is in the mobility sector. Generation Y are famously reluctant to buy cars. As they approach the legal age to drink alcohol, go to war and vote, these 'digital natives' are quite different from the previous generations. These Gen Ys learned to digitally interact soon after birth and demand their products be designed differently than, say, products meant for the Baby Boomer generation. This generation learned to text well before they were old enough to learn to drive. So driving is seen as the inconvenient obstacle to texting or being online with a smart device. Most adults (us included) can remember their first car: a product that symbolised freedom, independence and social status. It meant that we were mobile—able to go where we wanted, when we wanted. Today such teenage status is created very differently, online.

In Australia, there are laws preventing texting while driving. Engaging with a mobile device is seen as a distraction to the driver. However, Google contends that texting is not the distraction—driving is! They are introducing the autonomous vehicle—more evolution than revolution, really, when you think about it. The latent customer needs of this new generation are met by the birth of smart mobility. Figure 2.10 (overleaf) illustrates the changing meaning of driving.

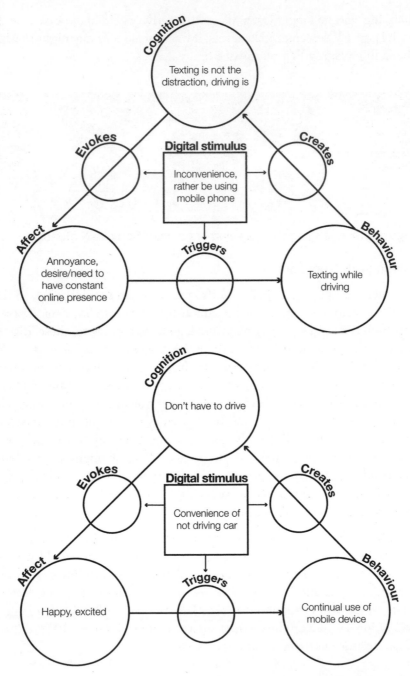

Figure 2.10: change in meaning of driving: inconvenience, the perceptions of driving (top), vs convenience, the perceptions of autonomous vehicles (bottom)

THE DIGITAL HEDONIC AFFECT

As previously explained, 'hedonism' is the doctrine that pleasure is the highest good; it's used to describe the pursuit of pleasure and a lifestyle devoted to pleasure-seeking. Consumers experiencing and seeking pleasure through the attainment of a product is called 'consumer hedonics'.

In our connected world consumers have information readily available, a range of different purchase options, and are able to change brands or services at any given time digitally.

Online purchases are one of the most rapidly growing forms of shopping, and its growth rates are outstripping buying through traditional retail channels. In digital consumption, the consumer's interaction or contact with the organisation is purely through a technology platform. As face-to-face interaction is a central part in relationship development, its absence leads to a relatively poor customer experience. Online customers rely entirely on sight and sound, whereas in physical experiences all senses come into play.

However, digital consumption has many advantages, including not being constrained by distance and opening hours, that provide a higher level of convenience to customers. Companies need to understand the importance of the digital experience in the establishment of trust and relationships with customers. For example, responses via digital platforms are often unidentifiable, leading customers to question if the response is that of the company or that of an employee acting on behalf of the company. Responses may also differ between employees, leading to inconsistencies in communication.

To manage such issues, new technologies have been introduced to digital channels, such as automated responses. However, such interactions have led to more one-sided rather than two-sided communications due to the generic, impersonal responses. The speed of response and reaction to the customer's message can heighten a customer's perceptions of a company's interactivity. A positive perception of the interactivity of a company can give the consumer a positive impression of its functionality and overall experience. The development of new technologies, such as wearable computing (including Google Glass, discussed in chapter 4) will continually change the way customers interact with companies, gain information and make transactions.

Just like consumers shopping in a store, digital consumers expect pleasurable experiences while shopping online. Consumption is a social activity; however, it is also very personal. Emotional shopping involves feelings that surround fantasising, purchasing, procuring and even designing their own fashion (explored more in the Burberry case study in part II). In digital hedonic consumption, this is experienced via technology, including but not exclusive to the purchase, usage and overall experience online.

A challenge of digital hedonic consumption is creating hedonic experiences with a range of different products. An example of this is the difference between purchasing clothing and purchasing music online. Clothing would be classified as a 'high-hedonic' product due to its symbolic, experiential and pleasing properties. The process of buying clothing often requires the consumer to touch, feel and most likely try on the article. Colours and textile feel may also not be fully conveyed through digital technology, leading to uncertainty or disappointment once the article is received. Compare this to purchasing music online. It is a 'low-hedonic' product as it is a digital article, which does not require an experiential process in its purchase, but rather later, in the use of it.

Examples of high-hedonic items include two highly customisable products launched recently—Nike By You and Shoes of Prey. Both companies have a well-designed 3D digital platform in which to customise your shoes and model them realistically online. As far as designing your own shoes goes, it is a high-hedonic experience. Nike entered this space to tap into the collector mindset of those shoe fanatics sometimes known as 'sneakerheads' (explored in the Cj Hendry case study in part I). Shoes of Prey approaches a different demographic, allowing women to completely customise a pair of shoes (heel height, materials, strap size, toe design, etc.). A pair of Shoes of Prey heels will be delivered to your door in approximately four weeks, while Nike got this time down to 90 minutes in their New York (invite only) studio.

As more retail companies take this leap into the world of advanced customisation, the quality and function of the product itself must not be forgotten. In the case of Nike By You, there is a smaller choice of options (limited to a selection of graphics, colour schemes and text) to customise. The design is then digitally projected onto a blank pair of sneakers the customer is wearing in store to demonstrate the resulting look. The limited choices ensure the final product will be functional as well as aesthetically pleasing. For Shoes of Prey (as brilliant as this Australian retail innovation is) the personalised combinations can at times compromise the overall function of the shoe design.

Digital consumption can be transformed into a type of entertainment, allowing digital consumers to devote their leisure time to searching for a range of products online. Designing experiences that are hedonic can increase the likelihood of engagement. Technological advancements make it possible to translate multisensory inputs such as colour and music online. These influence the level of pleasure felt by the consumer, generating a positive attitude and directly influencing the digital consumption.

A consumer's hedonic choice is the decision made to purchase a product for the enjoyment, pleasure and excitement it affords. In a digital environment, which lacks many of the cues for hedonic purchases, external justifications, such as targeted promotions, sales and exclusive discounts can encourage a hedonic purchase decision. Examples of this are discount codes and exclusive sales for online members. There are different levels of interactivity, from digital screens to virtual fitting rooms, however just like customising a pair of shoes, the digital experiences should always be a balance of enjoyment and functionality.

In a digital context, the experience must cultivate a relationship in the mind of the consumer. The use of digital channels for browsing increases a consumer's awareness of the product, service or promotion as well as their chance of purchasing through it. Equally, if someone has a positive experience buying online, it will also have a positive effect on their shopping activity as their confidence in the internet will be high and they will perceive less risk in purchasing through multiple channels. Here lies the opportunity to influence decisions with positive hedonic experiences across multiple channels simultaneously.

Avoiding digital hedonic temptations could be more challenging for consumers due to technological advancements that enable individually targeted advertising. Hedonic responses in this context become more important in consumer purchase decisions than utilitarian criteria. The immediate 'real-time' response that the online world can easily replicate (the gratification of purchasing at any time, anywhere) holds many implications for impulse purchases. In addition, more leisure time is spent browsing digital channels now than ever before, uncovering more opportunities to trigger hedonic experiences through such interactions.

FROM NOKIA TO APPLE

Hedgehogs are operation oriented, process driven and vital in managing an effective team. They don't miss anything—they have high standards, drive home compliance and are brought in to cut the fat. (They usually make the best engineers.) Nokia are a typical Hedgehog, as they were one of Finland's most famous exports for many years (with a history dating back to 1865). They were a heavily operational-driven organisation.

In the early 2000s, Nokia were a large player in the mobile telecommunications device industry. Their many handset designs helped them dominate the market. Flip phones were produced in every colour imaginable, creating an entirely new market for personalised casings. Product design was the majority of the design portfolio at Nokia's research headquarters.

However, their inability to progress past the physical design of hardware into a service offering was evident with the unsuccessful launch of their internet service, Ovi. They eventually sold the handset division to Microsoft in 2014. Other major reasons for Nokia's demise include an indecisive management team, destructive internal competition and the failure to forecast the impact of the smartphone. By 2007 Nokia had designed, manufactured and released over 307 different handsets, and they were losing their market position. Conversely, once the Apple iPhone hit the market in 2007 it went from strength to strength, despite the product design being very simple, with limited changes between the few new product releases.

Nokia were operationally driven and a victim of their own success. They got comfortable making incremental changes and defending their market position rather than disrupting it. They lost the ability to look to the future and the opportunities it held—much like Kodak.

In contrast is Steve Jobs' 'lovemark', Apple. A lovemark goes beyond the creation of a brand to build a symbol for people to fall in love with due to the experience it creates. The product, the packaging, the marketing messages and the physical retail experience are consistent. While others (such as Nokia) can try and compete on a product level, they are unable to provide the same customer experience as Apple in the Western markets in which they created this lovemark (see figure 2.11).

Figure 2.11: Nokia and Apple: two approaches to the mobile market

THE PERSONALITY OF OUR POSSESSIONS

Consumers can create meaning through the process of personalisation (as seen in Nike By You and Shoes of Prey), as through this process the consumer changes the functionality, interface or content of a system to increase its personal relevance. Possessions are especially important for personal identity, as they are a way for an individual to symbolically define and express who they are. By injecting meaning into products consumers own and view as valuable, they are able to display a piece of themselves through that stimulus. Therefore, possessions have value for their role in expressing or reinforcing the 'sense of self', especially when the product has had an influence or effect on the individual's personal history.

Strong emotions, memories and enjoyment during use can also contribute to the level of attachment an individual feels towards certain objects. This is seen when we become attached to certain objects while others remain easily disposable. Memories the individual associates with an object — for example, a clock that has been passed down from a deceased grandmother — also influence their level of attachment.

An emotional bond between consumer and product can be created before it is purchased, as products can elicit a range of emotional responses. It is this emotional attachment that determines the success or failure of a product. The immediate response of the user to the sensory aspects of a product is known as 'visceral design'. It has the power to immediately make consumers feel good about the product they are about to purchase, even before they have attached any specific emotions to it. There is a demand for hedonic benefits or a positive emotional response and experience when using a product.

Visceral design is achieved by designing products that focus on the emotional responses and experiences of the consumer instead of focusing purely on functional aspects of the product. The effort invested, whether mental or physical, when personalising a product is a major contribution to the bond between the consumer and the object. When mental effort is invested into personalisation (for example, choosing flattering colours), the level of attachment is greater than if purely physical effort was expended (such as putting together IKEA furniture).

This process has been referred to as 'consumers becoming co-designers', and it has an impact on the level of attachment and emotional value of an object. Permitting the consumer to make design decisions and be involved in the design process can also enhance the customer experience. Many companies are beginning to offer mass customisation of products online by allowing customers to either select or eliminate certain design criteria to suit their needs. This design technique offers more variety and has the possibility to expand a customer base. Research has also found that the types of consumers who value the opportunity to custom design products are willing to pay more. Mass customisation does not necessarily have the same benefits as personalisation, however, as it relinquishes a certain amount of design authority.

* * *

The term 'emotion' has long been used as a somewhat vague word to describe a wide range of affective phenomena considered to be irrational and external to rational decision making. However, research conducted on emotion in the fields of medicine, psychology, computer science and product design have firmly posited emotion as central to the cognitive reasoning process. Additionally, emotion is an integral and inescapable part of everyday life, involving the individual's engagement with the physical world. A consumer's emotions have a significant impact on purchase and consumption decisions.

The aim of this book is not to debate what emotions are, but to understand how the theories of emotions (regarding psychology, design and marketing) can be used to design digital channel engagements.

Consumers and designers operate in different spheres. The consumer must evaluate and interpret a product's beauty, function and message through interaction with its physicality, their experience with similar products, and within the environment of the consumer-product meeting. A designer may only communicate their intended design message via a product's physical manifestation.

In this context, the 'affect coding scheme' is used to identify emotions, moods and feelings (more on this in chapter 4) for the designer (source) to communicate through the medium of the stimuli (transmitter) to the consumer (receiver) — as shown in figure 2.8 (see p33).

This has strong inferences for the design of stimuli aimed at diverse user groups. Those who are new to the product, service or system are more susceptible to the affective elements of the digital product, while those more familiar tend to discount or even disdain affective cues. By harnessing the consumer relationship and using product rhetoric to design for positive emotional states, designers can increase the odds of the consumer receiving the intended message.

The next chapter shifts gears away from the internal state of consumers into the digital world of channels and all their complexity.

Cj Hendry: Art through Instagram

In this case study, we introduce you to the young female Australian artist—Catherine Jenna, aka Cj Hendry (whose work can be seen on the front cover of this book). She successfully (and exclusively) used the digital channel of Instagram to introduce her art to the world. Her big break came when an Australian art collector saw one of her images on Instagram in 2013. Within the short period of three years she had established herself in New York, having sold her art to such clientele as Kanye West. The path to success has been fast as she gained a cult-like following due to the global reach of social media. Cj has also received attention from many art critics condemning her work. However, with over 299 000 followers, her meteoric success was this study's motivation. We look at the strategy behind her operation and her ability to engage her audience through the use of her only digital channel: Instagram.

UNDERSTANDING THE ART INDUSTRY

Throughout the twentieth century, only a small minority of artists made a living from their craft—and only a handful over the entire century became financially well off from it. Why? Because they created a very successful business around their name (their brand) as well as their art, creating unique artwork but, more importantly, a unique business model that supports them. They are part entrepreneur. The most talented artists are very rarely the best paid.

Damien Hirst is reported as being one of the richest artists in the word, with wealth assessed in 2010 at £215 million (AU$363 million). He understood the business model of the art industry during the 1990s, but since then his stocks have been falling. He argues that artists should make their work the most expensive at the first point of sale, because a work of art is a 'product' that, much like a new car, depreciates in value as soon as it leaves the showroom. Artists never profit from auction resales, so Hirst argues that 'the first time you sell something is when it should cost the most'.

Traditionally, most individuals and companies have purchased art via galleries, brokers and publishing catalogues. This distribution model results in an inherently slower market. Artists and consumers also aren't receiving the best price due to auctioneers charging a 10 per cent commission, in addition to gallery fees of up to 50 per cent on top of the sale price. This market is different from others due to fixed supply, fluctuating market conditions and uncertainty over price and quality.

The value of the global art business is near US$66 billion with continuing strong growth, increasing by 8 per cent in 2014 alone. Online sales are a small but rapidly growing segment of the art market, generating €2.5 billion in 2013. In 1999 Amazon partnered with Sotheby's to run an online auction site for art, and eBay bought America's third largest auction house, Butterfield & Butterfield, to sell upscale art. This was the beginning of art's 'big bang' in an online environment.

Those who operate art-related businesses frequently have altruistic motivations for starting when compared to owners of other traditional profit-centred businesses. This commitment to creativity and personal goals can uniquely influence the marketing and operational style of the business. Artists can differentiate themselves from larger retailers who offer more standardised product assortments, and smaller retailers perform better with more innovative, more unique and higher-quality product lines. This illustrates that the internet and development of digital channels are offering innovative opportunities for artists to engage with a wider audience than has been traditionally available.

Online art purchasing faces several challenges, such as the authentication of the artwork and the fact the artwork can only be viewed on a digital screen. Most commercial, offline purchases of art are a combination of a social event, a public contribution and an intellectual exchange. In buying, the collector (the purchaser) creates an emotional bond with the artist, funding the further creation of art with their purchase. The experience is, however, changing due to art being sold online; dealers have closed stores in favour of art showcases and exhibitions for privileged audiences, leaving digital channels to be used to discover, curate, share and buy artworks and become the new curators in the art industry. The art industry could be compared to luxury brands in their use of digital channels as a way to create awareness of an aspirational brand value. These two industries also root their success in the scarcity and exclusivity of their product offerings.

With this perspective, digital channels can be leveraged to increase the knowledge and interest of potential buyers and create a wider audience for artists. However, there is limited research to explain how this is done.

THE ARTIST: CJ HENDRY

Cj Hendry is a photorealistic artist, creating artworks through a 'scribbling' process. Her story has been followed closely by the media over the last few years as her artwork has gained a strong following online. She admits to spending 14 hours a day drawing, so she has produced many collections of work in a relatively short period of time. These collections range from luxury goods to shopping bags to food items on a plate. One thing that all these pieces have in common is a distinctive attractive style that creates attachment and is difficult to ignore.

Cj has drawn media attention over the years, some of it more positive than others, and there has been much debate over her status as an artist. Regardless of this media debate, we included this case because of Cj's use of a single digital channel. One well-thought-out, well-considered, well-designed affective channel: Instagram. (We clarify the use of the term 'well' here: there is no denying her success, reflected in the sheer number of followers and the sale prices of her artwork.) She clearly is the proof that you don't need to be an art critic to define success in this field. Our research was collected during her rise to fame and began with the very first series of work she displayed, in Sydney in 2014.

COMMUNICATING A NEW MEANING

Cj has stated,

> Art to me is wanting to feel comfortable ... Art to me is something warm, engaging, understandable, interactive, something that everyone — not just art critics, not just art dealers, not just art curators understand. It's for everyone.

A love of art but bad experiences at art galleries and exhibitions led Cj to make her art approachable and accessible to everyone, making people feel like they can comment on and share in the artwork. She likened the experience of an art gallery to walking into a luxury-brand store, explaining it as 'uncomfortable' due to 'cold staff' creating the experience of being out of place. So when she changed her lifestyle to do what she loved, drawing, it made sense to pick Instagram as her only channel to publish her art. She states that Instagram

> is so interactive because everyone from every walk of life, every age, everyone can get the free account. They can look at it and view it and be a part of it. I think it should be for everyone. That's what art is.

Her online strategy is all about 'getting eyeballs onto the art', and wanting people 'just to go wow'. Her content is centred on making people feel a part of her artwork. She explains that, personally, she 'likes to see how it's done, and how it started, and I think people want to see that too'. Therefore, she posts a range of process photos and short time-lapse videos of her process, explaining,

> You need to bring people into the experience, to feel. I really think people buy because of the feeling. It's so much about the experience, the viewing ... People feel a part of it. People are like, 'I've seen it happen'. It's like you go through the process with the artist, the ups and the downs.

Many of Cj's artworks are drawings of luxury products, such as Chanel handbags and Hermés china. She relates this to wanting 'to bring it back to the luxury element and still make it free for everyone'. Overall Cj wants 'people to respect what I do and I think that's something really important — respect and admiration, lust for what I'm doing' as seen in figure A.

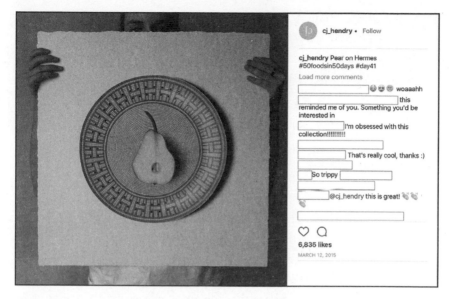

Figure A: sample of Cj_Hendry Instagram post, likes and comments

THE RISE OF INSTAGRAM

Instagram is a mobile app that publishes photos and videos, allowing users to capture and share their life moments with others. Instagram describes using the app as a

> fun and quirky way to share your life with friends through a series of pictures. Snap a photo with your mobile phone, then choose a filter to transform the image into a memory to keep around forever. We're building Instagram to allow you to experience moments in your friends' lives through pictures as they happen.

Launched in October 2010, it has attracted more than 400 million users, with approximately 80 million uploads per day. Similar to Twitter and other social channels, on Instagram individuals can follow other users and view their shared photos, effectively creating an audience for these images. The top hundred global brands use Instagram for brand awareness and management purposes, as it has an engagement rate

15 times greater than Facebook. Brands that advertise on Instagram report a 32 per cent increase in ad recall rates and 10 per cent increase in brand message recall.

Instagram has three advantages for business:

1) It's a major social channel that was launched on mobile phones rather than the internet, so users can access it anywhere.

2) It is visceral and is not as conversation-intensive as websites, Facebook or Twitter.

3) Posted content can be scrolled through quickly.

Social channels such as Instagram, Facebook and Twitter have allowed users to design their own brand, creating symbolic meaning and values through what they publish online.

There have been plenty of other artists who engage in the same visceral posting styles as Cj. However they do not have the same amount of followers, or the same amount of press coverage. So why is it that Cj has been so successful at mastering this digital channel?

ONLINE POST ANALYSIS

To answer this we analysed Cj's Instagram content (posts and comments) from December 2013 to June 2015, including all the photographs and videos posted on her profile, as well as the number of 'likes' and comments made. The purpose of this was to capture both the source (post) and the response (comments) and code these into emotions to understand the indicators for digital behaviours. During this time period a total of 541 photographs and video posts were collected from Cj Hendry's Instagram. For this analysis, the subject matter of the photograph was described; it was then coded into a descriptor, such as 'a piece in process' or 'a finished piece'; and we also recorded if the image was black-and-white or colour. A coding protocol was developed based on previous content analysis investigations, and research conducted by us. The following variables were included:

- date of the post
- number of likes
- number of comments
- post caption

- type of post (photo or video)
- content of the post.

Table A shows the post variables in more detail.

Table A: post variables

Post variable	Description
Content type	Content was posted as an image or video
Content agility	When the post was published (in weeks ago)
Content composition	Content was posted in black-and-white or colour composition
Content subject matter	Subject matter of post was categorised into 12 subjects, including: miscellaneous artefacts, sporting equipment, materials, guns, 50 foods, playing cards, artist photographs, luxury, skeletal, 100 dollar bill, country item and clothing items
Content descriptor	At what stage the art is being posted, including coding into five categories: finished piece, process, exhibition, frames and other
Response variables	**Description**
Likes	Number of likes a post received
Affect	Comments were coded using the affect eliciting conditions (seen in chapter 2, table 2.1), an emotion-code index based upon Desmet (user tags [@] and hashtags [#] were not included in this analysis)

USER RESPONSE ANALYSIS (COMMENTS)

We collected the likes and comments from the 17 most popular posts, taking out all comments that were links, spam or chain messages and keeping only plain text content. These formed the raw data for this stage of the study and a selection of 2334 comments were extracted for classification. A classification scheme was constructed to code the comments into emotions using the affect eliciting conditions, a coding index based upon Desmet's eliciting conditions (see table 2.1 in chapter 2). This coding aims to analyse emotions within written text via digital channels.

Businesses are able to gain instant customer feedback from digital channels; however, the emotions beyond what is written are important to gain a true understanding of their opinions. With affect coding we aim to identify emotions in text on digital channels; and to associate this with the value proposition of the company. Table B shows an example of an affect index.

Table B: example of affect index

Affect	Eliciting condition	Excerpts from comments
Admiration	Approving of someone else's praiseworthy action	Inspirational, amazing, epic, brilliant, captivating, unique, awesome, fabulous, gifted, breath-taking, unbelievable, talented, thankful, impressed, incredible, in awe, master, respect, dig, extraordinary, magnificent, freaky, speechless
Desire	An object calls for possession or usage	Custom ordering, purchase wanted, favourite, obsessed, must have this
Stimulation	A promise for understanding through exploration or a new action	Improvement, curious
Satisfaction	An expected goal realisation	Insane, mind blowing, crazy, amazing
Enjoyment	Liking a desirable or pleasant event	Woo, so excited, can't wait, dope, bravo, nice
Pleasant surprise	An unexpected goal realisation	Holy bananas
Love (liking)	Liking an appealing object	Beautiful, aesthetically pleasing, gorgeous, cute, crush, stunning

From the top 2334 comments we were able to 'decode' Cj's secret to engaging her audience. The emotional responses were categorised as follows:

- 45 per cent admiration
- 23 per cent stimulation

- 18 per cent enjoyment
- 8 per cent desire
- 5 per cent love
- 1 per cent pleasant surprise.

This indicates that posts that showcased a finished piece, the process or the exhibition Cj made increased the amount of admiration and stimulation comments received. Posts showing works in progress created a large sense of stimulation, as followers then anticipated the final product being uploaded. A short period of anticipation for the final reveal of the artwork created a lot of admiration. This became a pattern of behaviour that her followers came to know well—a formula, if you like. First she would upload an image of the subject of her next piece, then she would show the process and then the final finished piece—at times with a time-lapse video.

UNDERSTANDING EMOTIONS AND BEHAVIOURS

You need to bring people into the experience, to feel it. I really think people buy art because of the feeling. It's so much about the experience and the feeling you get while viewing it.

Cj Hendry

Through her strategy of translating her personal values and views of art into her Instagram account, Cj has been able to connect her value proposition of wanting 'art to be experienced by everyone'. Through her content, she has formed a relationship with the audience, eliciting an emotional connection from the concept to the finished artwork. In this case the digital channel of Instagram works due to the visceral response viewers get when they view her work. It immediately allows the audience to discover, curate, share and buy her artwork.

Figure B illustrates that cognition (what we think), emotion (what we feel) and behaviour (what we do) are related and influence each other—the Digital Affect Framework (as we discuss in detail in chapter 5). Through the use of Instagram, Cj Hendry has been able to build her personal brand, keeping a consistent posting style of black-and-white photos and videos.

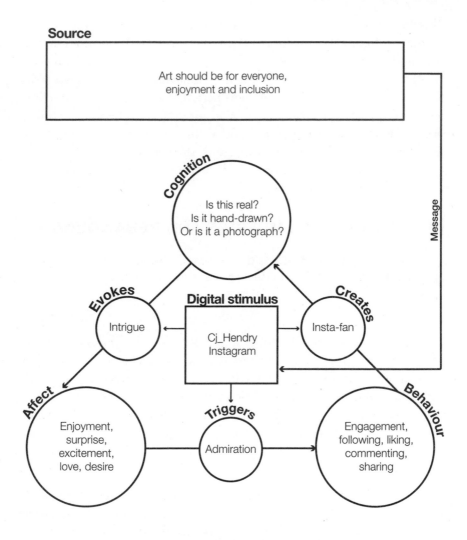

Figure B: Cj Hendry Digital Affect Framework

Cognition

The first response of the viewers is shock. They questioned whether what they were looking at was hand-drawn or if it was a photograph. They displayed different levels of disbelief in regard to this at first, and only after Cj uploaded time-lapse videos did the disbelief turn to intrigue about how she did it. These different attitudes and the change in perception towards the work resulted in a more powerful emotional response from the viewer.

Affect

The response was overwhelmingly positive: sheer admiration, desire to own one of her pieces, excitement in anticipating when the next post would be (in order to see the drawing evolve). Finished pieces of artwork, even though they were posted less frequently than process posts, received the most likes and shares. Using a variety of posting types and descriptors elicited greater overall engagement from users, as illustrated by the finished posts receiving more comments of admiration.

Behaviour

At the beginning, she tried to build that relationship and responded to her followers' questions, but as they rapidly grew the free time she had to dedicate to this dwindled. Understanding the indicators of audience emotions through online behaviours (comments, liking and sharing) has led her to get real audience feedback in real time to make strategic decisions in regard to her next collection, or subject matter choice.

The positive and negative #sneakerdead

In a project named '#sneakerdead', Cj took a pair of Nike Air Mag sneakers (the shoes worn by Marty McFly in *Back to the Future Part II*) and dipped them into black paint (figure C, overleaf). This action caused a large backlash through the internet, with a number of sneaker blogs criticising her. This project stirred many emotions from her Instagram audience, ranging from rage to admiration.

cj_hendry

Follow

cj_hendry #sneakerdead #butthead

I must give credit to Creative Recreation for
their paint dipped Cesario XVI's back in
2011. @theshoesurgeon for dipping his
Jordan 4's and dipping many many others.
More recently @sean_wotherspoon for his
red dipped Jordan Supremes. Thank you to
all the 100's of other sneaker dippers I have
not mentioned, I wasn't the first and
certainly won't be the last but I want you to
know you have inspired me!

Load more comments

5,169 likes

NOVEMBER 4, 2015

Figure C: #sneakerdead video of paint dipping

After dipping the shoes in the black paint (see figures C and D), she proceeded to throw them out with the rubbish on the footpath outside her New York studio. This act on such a sought-after and culturally significant shoe caused many negative comments (as documented in posts), but also received positive comments, especially when the artwork was auctioned for US$130 000 with 100 per cent of the sale being donated to the Sheltering Arms youth charity, with more than 900 pairs of shoes given to underprivileged children.

cj_hendry 1 of 2 #sneakerdead

I must give credit to Creative Recreation for their paint dipped Cesario XVI's back in 2011. @theshoesurgeon for dipping his Jordan 4's and creating other insane masterpieces. More recently @sean_wotherspoon for dipping his Jordan Supremes. Thank you to all the other creative sneaker dippers out there, I wasn't the first and certainly won't be the last but I want to thank you for inspiring this piece.

13,782 likes

NOVEMBER 9, 2015

Log in to like or comment.

Figure D: first look at the #sneakerdead artwork

We deconstructed the #sneakerdead campaign using the Digital Affect Framework where both positive and negative comments were catalogued, as shown in figure E (overleaf). As mentioned earlier, the first major finding was the popularity of finished pieces of artwork—even though they were posted less than process posts, they received the most likes and shares. The next major finding was the importance of posting a variety of photo types and descriptors, as following this posting style elicited greater overall engagement from users, illustrated in the finished posts receiving more comments of admiration.

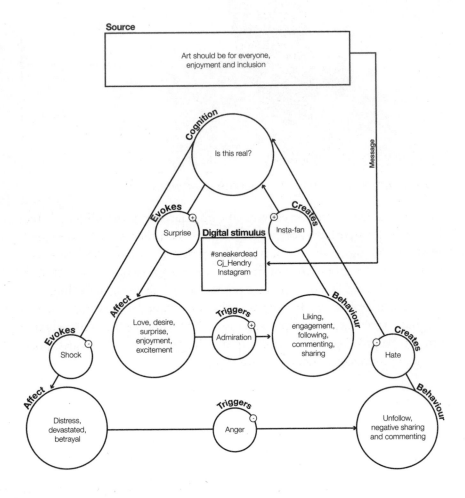

Figure E: the positive and negative affect of #sneakerdead

Cognition

The video of Cj herself dipping this expensive limited edition sneaker in black paint caused shock and surprise in many of the audience members. Many did not think it was the real item, that she would not dare to do something so bold, so reckless, so offensive.

Affect

This left some viewers devastated, betrayed and distressed at what was done to the exclusive shoe. The post containing the photo of the sneakers left in the trash on the side of the road sparked outrage, anger and hate mail. Many, however, were excited to see what would come next as she had never before drawn an item dipped in paint—the object selected to draw in this case was just as exclusive as the luxury brand items she had drawn before.

Behaviour

Some followers boycotted her Instagram and unfollowed her online. The underground sneakerhead subculture was most outraged and made its hatred for her and her art well known and public online. Others were ambivalent about the whole controversy and were excited to see the final drawing posted online and the subsequent charity auction of the piece.

LESSONS LEARNT: DESIGNING A DIGITAL CHANNEL

This case study of Cj Hendry taught us much in regard to the design of one channel. If we can apply these learnings, and align all channels to the core digital strategy (source) then we can start to make sure there is emotional alignment for consumers.

One of the strengths of Cj's approach was the detail to which she went in posting a range of shots of the process to the finished product. This process engaged the audience by taking them along the journey of the artwork's creation; it was truly art for everyone to enjoy.

These posts would have required thought, preparation and planning in order to execute them correctly. The entire channel also has a distinct style, monochrome only—and rarely showing Cj herself. On the downside, this reliance on Cj's own stylistic flair and creative expression makes this difficult to outsource.

As art was the product at hand, Instagram was the perfect channel. The visceral impact of the work stands out on this channel, and it has been a large part of the global effect she has had. It has allowed followers to interact with the artwork in its creation (by commenting and tagging Cj) and feel a part of the process. The time-lapse videos demonstrate transparency and viewers enjoy watching the piece of art take shape.

The captions on the posts at times caused confusion. The captions that are usually present next to a piece of art on the walls of a gallery are very carefully considered. They attempt to make sense of the complex piece of art they describe. Anyone who has met Cj or has seen her TEDX talks knows she has attitude, and her at times sarcastic style can be misunderstood. Often there was too much detail in the captions and there were misinterpretations, things getting lost in translation. The lesson here is to make sure the visual and the textual support each other in linking aligned emotion.

Key lessons from Cj Hendry

- Deliberately plan: understand the emotion you want to elicit.
- Ensure your style is consistent and thoughtful.
- Choose your channel wisely and play to its strengths.
- Align your visuals and text to best engage your audience.
- Create a distinct visceral aesthetic style to match your brand.
- Keep in mind the chronological order/sequence in which your posts will be seen.
- Design the posts collectively/holistically as an emotional experience for the audience.
- Keep your messages consistent with your core values.
- Check how each post reinforces the emotional/digital hedonic rhetoric of the company.
- Respond to and engage with the audience of your channel.
- Bring the audience along on the journey.
- Use the information the audience posts and the questions they ask to better understand what it is they are responding to and why.

- Leverage the comments as a timely source of customer insights.

- Use the posts strategically to prototype early new product propositions with the audience.

- Take your time and craft something meaningful in one post rather than less time on multiple posts.

- Quality posts over quantity posts is key.

PART II

Affective companies

CHAPTER 3

Digital connections: Stimulus, channels, touchpoints and typologies

This chapter introduces the world of digital channels and how companies should select them carefully.

In today's digital landscape, capturing the moment has almost become the only way to prove that the moment even existed (see figure 3.1, overleaf). Digital trends in our society have allowed us to access data and information worldwide, communicate without boundaries of time or place, and make multiple transactions in real time. With the number of internet users consistently increasing, so too are the number of digital channels and routes for communication.

In a world full of digital trends and digital moments, how can we embrace this new way of interacting and design for it? One way of doing this is to embrace the medium through which users interact with most businesses today—the digital channel. Digital channels are at the centre of communication between an organisation and its customers.

Figure 3.1: viewing the *Mona Lisa* in the Louvre, Paris, in the digital age

'Digital channels' is a collective term to describe technology-based platforms that use the internet to:

- connect with customers

- provide a range of different content and functions

- facilitate communication with a range of different levels of interaction.

This includes social media such as Instagram, Facebook and Twitter, content sites such as YouTube, and e-commerce, as well as company websites and advertisements on other sites. Digital channels demonstrate how the internet has changed and enabled entirely new forms of interaction and relationships between customers and companies.

'Relationship marketing' emerged in the 1990s and linked service marketing to the study of customer relationships and networks. User engagement issues, including such things as trust, communication, commitment and value, were researched in attempts to understand how relationships emerge and can be sustained. Research in the early 2000s explored behaviour variables in online communities, social influences and the effects of online word-of-mouth. The importance of online networking was recognised in 2006 by the Marketing Science Institute, which declared 'The Connected Customer' the top research priority. During this decade, digital engagement literature has been influenced by psychology and sociology, which has helped to decode the complexity and transparency of the internet.

Digital channels such as Facebook, Twitter and YouTube demonstrate that users are no longer just receiving data from corporations, but are actively engaging with, interacting with and even co-creating content. Customers are able to voice their concerns, contribute design ideas or request assistance, empowering them to broadcast positive and negative experiences with or without the approval of the company. Issues such as product quality, lack of availability, poor service and high prices are now transparent and instantly broadcast by the customer, often resulting in a loss of reputation, customers and revenue for the company. New digital channels, combined with increasing levels of digital literacy, also allow customers to become co-creators and co-producers with brands they engage with. Most companies are still unsure how to best seize the opportunities that digital channels present. The difficulty has not been in developing and launching their digital initiatives, but making them engaging and valuable to their customer base. Many companies implement digital channels with little or no strategic plan, simply driven by a fear of losing their competitive edge.

SeaWorld in the United States provides us with an example of how this can go wrong. In 2015, they tweeted an open question hashtag (#AskSeaworld) to encourage engagement, park visits and new fans. This was after the release of a documentary titled *Blackfish*, which alleged the amusement park engaged in animal rights abuse. The hashtag had the opposite of the intended effect: as animal rights activists took to Twitter and rebelled with the hashtag #EmptyTheTanks. Many kept reposting and responding to the original tweet with remarks about the treatment of the whales. Customers responded with contempt.

In another example from 2015, U2 made a deal with Apple to automatically download their new album, *Songs of Innocence*, to 500 million iTunes accounts, whether users wanted it or not. The attacks were instantaneous and unforgiving, and Bono later apologised, confessing that they 'might have gotten carried away…'. Many users closed their iTunes account, thinking they had been hacked.

These examples illustrate a disconnect between the source and the stimulus can lead to backlash and negative responses. This disconnect can be seen in figure 3.2 (overleaf).

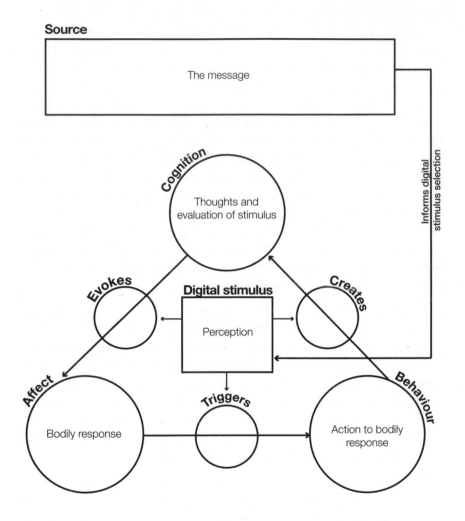

Figure 3.2: don't get lost in transmission: connecting the message and digital stimulus

REEBOK: HOW MANY IS TOO MANY?

Retail brand Reebok conducted audits of their digital channels over a two-week period in 2012. They discovered they had more than 600 company- and customer-created digital channels, including 232 Facebook pages, 30 Twitter accounts for different product lines, and 100 YouTube channels. Over 50 per cent of these were created by fans using the Reebok trademark. Reebok now have three Facebook pages, two Twitter accounts and one YouTube channel, all company created and controlled. This example (illustrated in figure 3.3) demonstrates how the rapid proliferation of digital channels can lead to an excessive online presence with little strategy. For customers, this multitude of channels is confusing, overwhelming and disjointed.

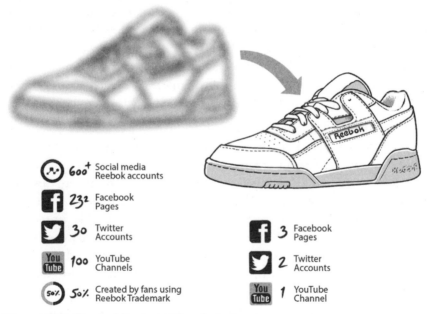

Figure 3.3: Reebok's streamlined strategy

FROM TRADITIONAL TO DIGITAL

'Channels' refer to the way a company 'goes to market' encompassing all customer contact points or the medium through which a company interacts with the customer. These avenues have been described as 'dynamic webs', as they comprise many direct and indirect ways to reach and service customers. A company's interface with customers plays an important role in the customer experience. Channels are not always digital, examples of physical channels include stores, catalogues, direct mail and dealer shows. However, a surge in 'technology-based self-service' is decreasing the role of a company's face-to-face interaction with customers. Digital channels deliver very different experiences compared to those provided through traditional physical or 'brick-and-mortar' channels as the customer's contact with the organisation is through technology, such as a website. Because of this, customers have to rely entirely on sight and sound, whereas in a traditional channel experience all senses come into play. However, digital channels have many advantages, such as not being constrained by distance and opening hours, and providing a higher level of convenience to customers. The main use of digital channels is as an information service, since the primary value exchanged between the company and consumer is information. Customers are now channel surfers, connecting with the company through both its physical and digital channels, meaning the various channels must all present a harmonious image and identity. The available channel options provide companies with a way to differentiate themselves, as each channel offers different coverage, expertise, performance and engagement possibilities.

To address this, companies are shifting towards a more customer-centred view when designing and managing channels. Traditionally, channels have been organised by the functions performed by a company's distribution system. These include the components of an organisation (manufacturers, wholesalers, distributors, retailers), that help make an offering available to the customer. Now channels enable immediate information retrieval and larger networks of customers witnessing all that goes on in a very public way. Channels are now created as a point for the conception, promotion and delivery of positive customer and brand experiences.

Traditionally, a customer would stay with one channel (e.g. retail store) until the purchase was made. However, with the increasing number of channels, today's customer has become detached from the channels that used to claim them. This is due to customers becoming more adversarial, strategic and informed. Customers can now search for information at one channel, purchase at the next and retrieve the product through another channel.

This has led customers to exploiting various channels to fulfil different parts of the buying process. Customers expect to be able to interact with a company at all times. They are referred to as the 'always on' customer, likely to search, enquire, interact, complain, buy and pay through digital channels. Therefore it is important to explore how customers behave through their entire experience with a company, and to question whether all their needs are being met.

As the customers of today use a variety of channels to fulfill different needs at different times, they may take advantage of a company's up-front information and support without necessarily making the purchase that the company counted on to subsidise this support. By operating multiple channels—digital, as well as physical—companies can cater to the evolving purchasing motives of their customers.

The key issue for a company is how it can best fulfil its customers' needs by offering different channels through which customers can engage and purchase. In order to do this, it is important to know how customers behave, including their motivations and their choice of channel usage.

IMPACT OF DIGITAL CHANNELS

As customers are more engrossed than ever with the online world, with many of us spending an average of eight hours a day interacting with technology, our expectations of companies are changing. An example of an industry that has seen user engagement radically change due to the internet and digitisation of content is traditional newspapers. The way we consume news has changed: stories have been shortened (often delivered in less than 140 characters), and we are able to add our own commentary and use social media to make a story go viral. Many of us regularly hear breaking news stories on social media before they break on mainstream sources.

Operating in this digital environment has led companies to become information-intensive, as opposed to being labour- and capital-intensive. Companies now have valuable intelligence when making strategic decisions.

Social media is a digital channel that has had an impact on all companies. Many marketers view social media as a means for dispensing promotional messages and offers. However, social media is intended, in the words of Facebook, to be a 'social utility that connects people with friends and others who work, study and live around them'. Figure 3.4 shows the wide range of industries that are amongst the 20 most liked companies on Facebook (as of June 2017).

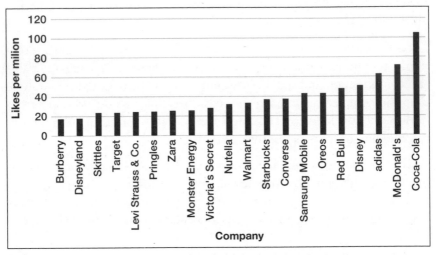

Figure 3.4: the most liked companies on Facebook

The use of social media as a way to engage with customers when they have a problem is well documented. However, companies should be aware that there are many more digital channels to select from and that the most important thing is to select the correct one for your intended message.

As seen in the Cj Hendry case study, how something is communicated via digital channels is as important as what is communicated. Figure 3.5 shows two examples of this: BlackBerry famously sent out an advertisement from an iPhone, and British Airways accidently promoted visiting London through a competitor's link.

Figure 3.5: channel fails: BlackBerry and British Airways

DIGITAL TOUCHPOINTS

We use the term 'digital touchpoints' to describe an individual digital channel (e.g. website), while the term 'digital channels' is used to describe a group of touchpoints (e.g. website, podcast, mobile app). Table 3.1 outlines 33 digital touchpoints, however this is not an exhaustive list due to the rapid addition of new touchpoints.

Table 3.1: digital touchpoint index

Apps	E-commerce retailers	Live Chat
Blogs	E-newsletters	Online Store
Competitions	Emails	Pinterest
Digital advertisements	Facebook	Podcasts
Digital campaigns	FAQs	Reddit
Digital catalogues	Flickr	Tutorials
Digital feedback forms	Forums	Twitter
Digital loyalty programs	Foursquare	Vimeo
Digital magazines	Google+	Web enquiry
Digital media releases	Instagram	Website
Digital memberships	LinkedIn	YouTube

In a study of 100 companies across 16 industries the most frequently used digital touchpoints were websites (100 per cent), Twitter (96 per cent), Facebook (94 per cent), YouTube (87 per cent) and LinkedIn (83 per cent). Figure 3.6 shows an in-depth breakdown of touchpoint rate of use.

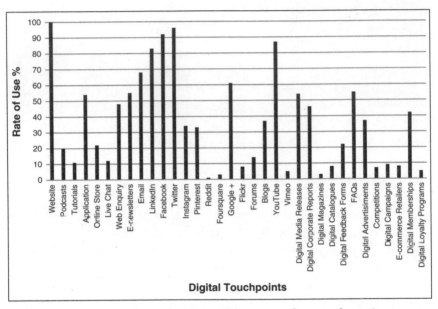

Figure 3.6: the digital touchpoints 100 companies used most

DIGITAL TYPOLOGIES

The results in figure 3.6 give us insight into what digital touchpoints companies are using, however this leads us to the question of which digital touchpoints are best suited to which company needs. To answer this question, we need to use the concept of 'digital typology'.

A digital typology is the grouping of digital touchpoints with common characteristics, such as the content displayed, the purpose, the direction of communication and how interactive it is (see appendix C for the full index of digital typologies and touchpoints). Four key typologies are explained in this chapter:

1. functional
2. social

3.   community

4.   corporate.

Functional typology

Most functional touchpoints have one-directional communication directed from the company to the customer. The two most frequently used functional digital touchpoints are website and email.

Websites are usually a customer's first point of interaction with a company, and they are usually directed to it from an internet search or advertisement. The content displayed varies from website to website, as does the design. Most websites have information on store locations, opening hours, contact details, customer service options and careers.

There is also a relationship between different touchpoints in this typology, such as the connection between the website and emails. Generally, the connection of these two touchpoints begins with the customer being directed to the website, where a purchase is made or they subscribe to an email newsletter. This interaction sends information to the company in real time, triggering a prepared response that continues their conversation with the customer. Most of these emails provide links back to the website. The frequency and content of emails also varies; high frequency of emails (over one per week) can become excessive, leading to customers unsubscribing. However, emails can offer exclusive promotions to subscribed users, which increases customers' willingness to stay subscribed.

Some companies use incentives to subscribe via the website, for example offering deals such as '15 per cent off your next shop'. The constant interaction between website and email should be used to drive traffic to the website, providing exclusive promotions or information to those subscribed. These emails are referred to as 'transactional emails', automatically generated to increase traffic between touchpoints, such as sending a reminder that items are still in your shopping cart, or a 'wish list' item is on sale, or rewarding subscribers with special deals for signing up. Kate Spade is one example of a company that delivers on-brand personalised emails and trolley reminders to customers at regular intervals (see figure 3.7, overleaf).

Figure 3.7: connecting touchpoints: Kate Spade's personalised email

Social typology

Social touchpoints are those run by an administrator with the ability to delete messages and block users. All social touchpoints are highly interactive, with two-way communication and the ability to post and respond directly to comments in real time. However, limited company activity in these touchpoints can lead to a high level of customer-created content, as shown in the Reebok example in figure 3.3 (see p71).

Social touchpoints provide the opportunity to gain customer feedback instantly. Each social touchpoint offers value through providing relevant customer content (e.g. Facebook feedback through comments, Twitter news and complaints platform, Instagram updates through photographs, Pinterest mood boards for inspiration). On average, companies create four social media touchpoints, providing information on the company background, contact information and opening hours. However, many lack integration and consistent activity across these touchpoints.

Most companies are capable of creating posts on average three to four times a week; however, they do not engage with user comments on posts or reply to site comments. These comments are usually a question in regard to a product or service, or a complaint due to lack of information or inconsistency.

Social touchpoints are prevalent through social media, with many advertisements also linked to touchpoints via slogans such as 'like us'. Various social touchpoints also allow for sharing, such as linking Instagram posts to Facebook and vice-versa. Some companies encourage this engagement by asking customers to tag them in posts. Competitions have also emerged across social media touchpoints, asking customers to like, tag or hashtag to enter. This consistent presence keeps customers engaged and interested, increasing traffic between digital touchpoints.

Being active on digital channels is not limited to posting and responding to posts, but also understanding the interaction between physical products and digital campaigns, and being aware of the longevity of both. Heinz had a highly publicised social media fail when QR codes on their tomato sauce bottles led to a German porn site rather than the Heinz website. It turned out that Heinz registered the site but let the domain name expire once the campaign was done, leading to a social media fail (see figure 3.8).

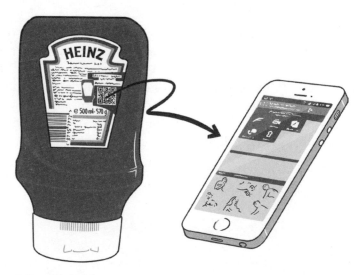

Figure 3.8: Heinz QR code fiasco

Community typology

Community touchpoints run and rely on a group of users. Users have the ability to remove content if it infringes copyright or is deemed inappropriate. The purpose of all touchpoints within a community is diversion, providing members with the ability to participate in recreational and social activities. YouTube, blogs, forums and Vimeo are touchpoints that allow for this through text, images and videos, with the ability for community members to comment and rate posts.

The interaction between the company and a select community of customers creates an opportunity for providing in-depth information and communication in specific interest areas. However, a lack of engagement or activity on these touchpoints can lead to disconnection and a loss of community. Most blogs and forums demonstrate interaction through asking questions, with many answers being provided by other members.

Rather than creating a physical community, companies are able to create digital communities by providing a personal and local connection. As like-minded customers engage via community touchpoints, they are able to share tips, provide support, photos and comments, creating a high level of customer-created content that can be shared via their personal digital touchpoints. Companies are able to form connections by communicating a lifestyle aligned with the company objectives, which is different to the social typology.

Whole Foods Market is a health- and environment-focused supermarket with blogs and forums run by the CEO and employees. Whole Foods forged a presence on Pinterest in mid-2011 because its community manager had over 300 000 followers. Posts include updates on charitable efforts, and promoting community and educational involvement, which provides unique support to each community that Whole Foods has a physical store in, as well as global support (see figure 3.9).

Figure 3.9: creation of a community: Whole Foods on Pinterest

The Pinterest boards are broader, to pull in people with a range of different interests, and in turn making the content more 'pinnable'. Further, they encourage local involvement through blogs, reinforcing their mission and creating transparency through blog content written by the owners, executives and customers. Essentially, they create a business about people, enabling the customer to feel as though they are a part of a community. The online Pinterest community has also grown to include access to monthly food prep workshops, where customers shop for a list of groceries and follow online via a video.

Corporate typology

All touchpoints in the corporate typology are one-way, require low to medium interaction and have a clear functional purpose. This one-way interaction is either from company to customer or customer to the company. The majority of these touchpoints play a supportive role to other touchpoints. Corporate touchpoints are capable of providing in-depth company information, leading to company transparency and trust, such as providing digital media releases, magazines and catalogues, including annual reports. Another aspect of corporate touchpoints is allowing customers the opportunity to provide feedback, ask questions or find an answer to a commonly asked question through either digital feedback forms or FAQs.

Giffgaff (see figure 3.10), a mobile virtual network operator, have their customer service online, proactively pushing information out to their notice board page. Through customer-generated tips and tricks and FAQs, the notice board creates a peer-to-peer support network for users, moderated by giffgaff employees. What sets this interaction apart is that users are given incentives to participate and contribute through Kudos points, a payback rewards scheme, and these points can then be either redeemed for pre-pay credit or donated to a charity. The use of these has resulted in 50 per cent of customer questions being answered via the community, with an average question response time of under three minutes and 95 per cent rate of questions answered within 60 minutes.

Figure 3.10: making less-corporate work: giffgaff peer-to-peer support

Table 3.2 outlines the criteria for the four typologies.

Table 3.2: the four types of digital touchpoints

Typology	Criteria	Touchpoints
Functional	Run by one user or company Medium to low customer interaction, commonly through the ability to post comments, email enquiries or set up chats	Website Podcasts Tutorials App Online Store Live Chat Web enquiry E-newsletters Emails LinkedIn
Social	Run by an administrator with ability to delete and block users High user interaction and ability to post and respond directly to comments in real time; limits on number of characters	Facebook Twitter Instagram Reddit Foursquare Flickr Google+
Community	Run by an administrator with features such as privacy settings Micro-bloggers can post longer forms of text, with a number of images and videos; customers can comment and rate the posts	Forums Blogs YouTube Vimeo Pinterest
Corporate	One-way engagement from company to customer or customer to the company No cross-interaction possible between company and customer	Digital media releases Digital magazines Digital catalogues Digital feedback forms FAQs Digital advertisements Competitions Digital campaigns E-commerce retailers Membership Loyalty programs

BENCHMARKING WITHIN AN INDUSTRY

Which typology is best suited to which business? To answer this question, we thought it best to benchmark industries to better understand their position in the market.

We conducted a study of 100 companies' use of digital channels to understand if a relationship between the four typologies and industries exists (see figure 3.11). The total number of touchpoints in each typology was recorded for each company; the average for each typology was then calculated for each industry. All industries correlated into two relationships: either 'functional and social' or 'functional and corporate'.

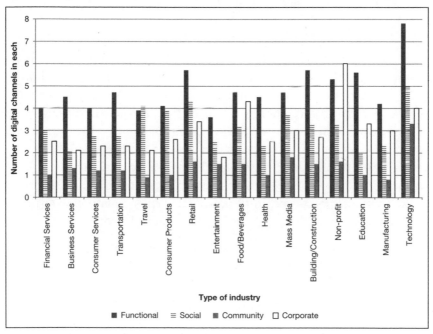

Figure 3.11: knowing where you fit: Typologies of different industries

Functional and social industries

Functional and social industries include financial services, consumer services, transportation, travel, consumer products, retail, entertainment, mass media, building/construction and technology. The use of these two typologies shows the main focus of these industries: promotion and revenue. The high interaction between functional and social touchpoints is evident through websites highlighting social touchpoints with 'connect with us' and social touchpoint icons. Functional touchpoints have the ability to engage through interactive media and publish news on products and campaigns, but they lack the ability to engage with users in the same manner as social media touchpoints. Therefore, the connections between these two typologies strengthen engagement with customers. A common connection included posting a new product via a social touchpoint, which then guided the customer to a functional revenue touchpoint—either the online store or website. Another common practice was highlighting special discounts for a limited time only for social media users, which again brought customers back to the functional touchpoint. The integration of these two typologies is one that many companies are aware of; however, it is often not optimised.

Functional and corporate industries

Functional and corporate industries include business services, food/beverages, health, non-profit, education and manufacturing. Combining these typologies gives you the ability to provide functional requirements, such as company information, while also offering access to the corporate reports required to build trust (an evident customer need within the exhibited industries). Non-profit companies had the highest rate of corporate touchpoints; this could be related to their need to build customer trust and confidence in the company's reliability and integrity. As all the touchpoints within the corporate typology are one-way, they require the customer to search for required information.

These typologies provide a guide for you to understand what is standard in your industry as a starting point.

SELECTING THE RIGHT CHANNEL

Many companies have a vast online presence, yet choose to be active on only a selected digital touchpoint or are inconsistently active across many of their touchpoints. By adopting a digital channel strategy, companies could become more responsive, delivering better customer service when and where assistance is needed. Customers should be considered active characters in the development of a company's digital channel strategy.

Channels are dynamic webs made of direct and indirect ways to reach and service customers. To reach and service the customer, we need to know their needs and requirements. Different typologies can address different customer needs:

- functional touchpoints provide, quick, accessible company information with the ability to respond to customer-directed enquiries

- social touchpoints allow for customer participation, sharing and collaboration, increasing the amount of information created; high engagement between customers and employees and customers to customers is also possible, however limited company activity can lead to high levels of customer-created content

- community touchpoints allow for engagement between a group of people with the same interests, allowing for in-depth information to be shared; however, a lack of engagement can lead to community being lost

- corporate touchpoints address customer needs such as accessing common customer questions and information on the company; limiting these touchpoints can lead to customers questioning the transparency of the company and losing trust.

Table 3.3 (overleaf) explores a range of customer needs and company objectives to direct the best touchpoint choice.

Table 3.3: customer needs and typologies and touchpoints

Customer content needs	Company objectives and key touchpoints				Typologies
	Information	Promotion	Support	Revenue	
Employee contact/ provide feedback	Email FAQs	E-newsletters Website	Email Web enquiry Digital feedback forms	–	Functional
Instant employee contact	Online chat	Facebook Twitter Instagram	Facebook Twitter Instagram	–	Functional Social
Company information	Website LinkedIn	Online advertising E-newsletters	FAQs Email	Digital advertisements	Functional Corporate
Purchase process	Website	Facebook Twitter Instagram	Online chat Email Web enquiry FAQs	Online store App	Functional Social
Community discussion (company-directed)	Blogs Forums YouTube App	YouTube Pinterest	YouTube Forums Blogs FAQs	Digital advertisements Competitions	Community Corporate

Instant company updates	Website Facebook Twitter Instagram Pinterest	Facebook Twitter Instagram Pinterest	Facebook Twitter	Website App	Functional Social
Shared interest	Pinterest Facebook Twitter	Digital catalogues Digital magazines	Pinterest Facebook Twitter	Website App Online store	Social Corporate Revenue
Community engagement (customer-directed)	YouTube Vimeo	Vimeo Pinterest Digital campaigns Flickr	Blogs Forums FAQs Digital feedback	Competitions E-retailers App	Social Community Corporate
Trust	LinkedIn Digital media releases Corporate reports	Digital catalogues Digital magazines	Blogs Forums FAQs	Membership Loyalty programs	Community Corporate
Company data/statistics	LinkedIn Digital media releases Corporate reports	Digital catalogues Digital magazines	FAQs Digital feedback forms	Membership Loyalty programs Digital advertisements	Functional Corporate

MULTICHANNEL CUSTOMER EXPERIENCES

Over the past decade, organisations have adopted increasingly complex digital communication strategies. However, practitioners' mindsets have yet to adapt, as digital channels are still approached in the same way as traditional communication, each used in isolation, rather than connecting and triggering communication across each other. In a truly efficient multichannel digital strategy, no channel stands alone.

By spanning the digital and physical realm, most customers are already multichannel users. Physical contact has advantages: it can create intimacy by reducing the disconnect between the retail staff and the customer, allowing for recurring encounters and a more complex and personal relationship to develop and mature.

On digital channels it is difficult to replicate those bonds. Frontline employees have the opportunity to react and adapt to a customer's needs based on their first-hand interactions, delivering the content and style required for each interaction. This also enhances communication between employees and customers as a customer's problems can be reviewed and addressed more efficiently.

As explained in chapter 2, the main concept that lies at the core of design is user experience, which requires treating the user holistically as a feeling, thinking, active person. Multichannel customer experiences include the interaction between the customer and the channel, which may include interaction with employees (e.g. in store) or via technological platforms (e.g. social media). Both design and multichannel strategies require a holistic understanding of the user to elicit an experience.

The pre- and post-experience strategies of these channels are just as important as the design of the channel itself. These strategies should all be designed holistically, as the pre-experience stage focuses on managing brand messages and the product or service's core customer, while the post stage focuses on reaffirming brand messages and making the customer return. The experience stage is the most vital and susceptible to the influence of a designer. Designers can create this through intended affect—influencing both the physical and relational aspects of the experience. However, designers in most companies are limited to stylistic afterthoughts such as colour, space and function, with only limited control over the emotional side of the design (usually handed downstream in a marketing brief).

CUSTOMER ENGAGEMENT THROUGH COMMUNITIES

Airbnb is a peer-to-peer digital engagement that enables the renting of personal property for accommodation to other members on the social network. Owners and visitors are enticed by a cheaper-than-average renting cost and a unique experience that hotel chains cannot provide. The Airbnb engagement starts on a digital platform but requires a level of trust between users due to the sharing of physical assets. This trust is facilitated through a rating system: the community promotes good service providers and filters poor performers.

Uber is a peer-to-peer ride-sharing service that connects drivers to passengers through a mobile app to provide a taxi-style service. As a driver or passenger you can decide when you would like to provide or consume the service. The mobile app connects people directly from its network of users, without the need for an asset-intensive broker.

Uber uses digital channels to forge a strong community that bridges online and physical interactions. These firms do what social channels indirectly accomplish and traditional players find cost intensive (i.e. have a company representative at every Uber trip or Airbnb key exchange). This is done through each firm's core channel. In the case of Uber, it is their app; with Airbnb, their app and website. This all-purpose channel is also each firm's main revenue stream, platform and marketplace.

The channel connects people online yet brings people together physically through the service delivery. Trust is generated through initial virtual interactions and user reviews and ratings. Immediately this community-created innovation puts Uber and Airbnb ahead of their industrial-era rivals purely through cost savings. However, to ensure this saving is viable and interactions continue, customers and transactions need further safeguards.

Although both companies provide insurance safety nets for providers and customers, little intervention is usually required. The community self-regulates solely through their digital channels. Below-average providers or customers are quickly rated down and filtered out or banned from the community.

The overall channel strategy of these two businesses is to direct customers to their core channel: their mobile app or website. Supporting channels primarily provide information and awareness of the brand and product in order to form the community.

CULTURE IS KEY

Digital channel design (as if it was not complex enough) also has to take the cultural landscape into account. One example of this is a German luxury automobile company we worked with back in 2011. They had designed an ad campaign that depicted an amazing luxurious driving experience, whizzing around scenic mountain roads at ridiculously fast speeds. However, when this product was launched in Beijing, their target market was not looking for the same driving experience. The automakers had failed to realise that anyone in Beijing who purchased a luxury car was more than likely to never go over 30 kilometres an hour in Beijing traffic, and their chauffeur would be the one to enjoy all the wood-grain detailing and beautiful leather driver's seat, while the buyer sat in the uncomfortable back seat!

What works for one market or culture is not the same for another. Here are a few more examples to demonstrate the difference of approach to digital channel design in different cultures.

Kate Spade: Japan micro-stores

Kate Spade made a tactical decision in Japan. They knew digital appetites could be different across cultures. Many organisations will roll out the same digital approaches worldwide and learn the hard way that cultural nuances can play a large part in customer motivations and attitudes. They decided to substitute in-store paper signage with iPads in their new micro-stores in Japan. This was done in order to deal with the tiny size of the stores. The retail footprint is a mere 93 square metres—too small to fit a permanent point-of-sale system. So they designed a modular system for displaying stock. But this made holding stock an issue, so they designed a compact and integrated supply chain so they would not have to hold stock (see figure 3.12).

Figure 3.12: Kate Spade's small Japanese stores are big on digital engagements

It made them wonder if customers would even visit a physical store anymore. So the intention of the iPads was to evoke positive stimulation through 'down-time'. Strategically, the micro-shop was less about selling to the customer and more about entertaining them, giving the shoppers a reason to come back and re-visit the store. If the customer wanted to know more, they could use the iPads to discover where the product was made, what inspired the design, and how it could be styled. And as all of this is digital, Kate Spade were able to update the information instantly and without the traditional restraints of a physical store.

Homeplus: Future of retail?

The first virtual store shelves for time-poor but productive South Korean commuters opened in 2011 at selective subway stations. Tesco's Homeplus was a visual experiment in mobile supermarket shopping. The store played on the known activity of shopping, with customers still approaching 'shelves' (2D images of supermarket shelves) to select items. QR code technology linked a digital customer profile to purchase orders. Once a purchase was confirmed, the customer could continue their day by immediately stepping onto the next subway service. The purchase order was quickly analysed, activating the vast distribution chain of Tesco within seconds. Deliveries were able to arrive in minutes or hours at the customer's discretion, rather than the days expected with other e-commerce services (see figure 3.13).

Figure 3.13: culturally aware: Homeplus approach to shopping in Korea

South Koreans are amongst the hardest working people (in work hours) in the world, often too busy to go shopping for groceries at a traditional store. And when they do so, the supermarket is often an overcrowded, painfully frustrating experience.

The virtual store prototype saw over 900 000 commuters download the app in less than one year, making it the most popular shopping app in South Korea. Online sales increased by 130 per cent after the introduction of the QR-coded subway station stores. They expanded its presence in South Korea, and the brand has since held the number one online retailer position in the country. They are now number one for online groceries not only in South Korea, but globally.

* * *

The ability to engage, act, interact and co-create online is the key characteristic of digital channels. Its ability to create closer relationships between the producer and consumer of content or services also distinguishes it from other platforms. Such success is explored in the next chapter, as it examines these digital channels within the realm of business strategy.

CHAPTER 4

Digital business: Success in a virtual world

So how can the field of design and emotion help leaders with developing digital channel engagements, delivering the online experiences that customers seek? Digital channel engagements can be better designed by starting with the emotional meaning or proposition of the company. Currently most companies rely heavily on either technology or product innovation to gain a competitive advantage; however, both technology and product innovation can be easily copied and quickly surpassed by competitors. Businesses need to think beyond innovation alone and to design strategies and avenues that work together to create a sustainable competitive advantage and deliver value to their customers.

Getting users to engage in digital stimulus requires an understanding of the different levels of engagement. It also requires thinking about how people use technology, the purpose of the content, and the needs of specific user groups. This chapter offers a framework to implement what has already been discussed in chapters 1 to 3: engaging customers meaningfully.

Design focuses on understanding user needs, and the information posted by users on digital channels can be a way to collect and understand these needs. By asking users to interact, rather than simply react to content, you can gain new insights and opportunities to design new products and services that will be successful (and profitable) in the global marketplace.

The current pace of change not only amplifies the need to more astutely address customer needs, but also to consider ways to gain value by providing new products and services.

In traditional equilibrium-oriented views of strategy, there is an assumption that there will be relatively little change in the constraints within which leaders operate. While innovation is high on leaders' agendas, most companies are still struggling with its successful implementation and integration into everyday practice.

Research suggests that approaching innovation through a dynamic, design-centred lens can create new perspectives that look beyond known assumptions, barriers and constraints. The integration of design into a company's culture and processes is also a way to innovate beyond the isolation of products, services and processes. Many organisations are still choosing to focus on their product or service, rather than on their customer and their overall experiences.

HEDGEHOG STRATEGY

A company's strategy is more than a signal of quality; it's also a way to communicate intangibles, for example, passion or excitement. Building honest relationships between the company and the customer is now paramount to success. Consumers are better informed than ever before, resulting in high expectations and low loyalty. As customers are becoming active members in digital channels, they also participate in creating company identity and building brand equity.

As organisations now employ a range of digital channels, more customers are participating in online dialogue, interacting with each other, co-creating their 'identity of self' through the identity of the brand. Consumers interact with brands in ways the organisation may not anticipate. Customer interaction is increasingly based on inputs provided by other customers and stakeholders, reaching beyond the control of the organisation.

Business engagements with customers can be strengthened by good design and management of a company's digital channels. Companies must have processes that allow them to create deeper engagements with their customers. When customers are not included in the design process products inevitably miss their market, in some cases with catastrophic consequences.

Google Glass (see figure 4.1) has been hailed as an epic failure in the marketplace in recent years. Some say they just launched it too soon—they were before their time. Others claim that, between the expensive price point (at US$1500 each), privacy issues and a cultural backlash, a connection with the marketplace was just never made.

Figure 4.1: an epic failure: Google Glass (2013–14)

The reported five main reasons for why Google Glass missed the mark are said to be:

1. health concerns about radiation exposure so close to your head

2. the aesthetics (it was ugly-looking)

3. confusion surrounding its readiness or whether it was just a prototype

4. it appeared to have no real function—what problem did it solve?

5. the channel to customers was difficult—it was not sold in stores, but rather exclusively through an early adopters' club.

The worst part was the negative campaign online caused by none other than the early adopters, the technology geeks, using the product for the first time and sharing their experiences on their social and personal channels. In hindsight, could designers have ironed out these issues before the launch? You bet!

This problem can be neatly illustrated by an episode of *The Simpsons* where Homer demonstrates a position that can at times be all too common amongst innovation managers, designers and marketers. He's invented a 'revolutionary make-up gun' for women who only have 'four-fifths of a second to get ready'. When Homer's daughter, Lisa, protests that the product won't work, Homer retorts 'Women will like what I tell them to like.'

This is similar to the Google Glass: the customer's emotional latent needs are missing from the equation. The paradox is that businesses spend far too much time perfecting their product offering (in this case a make-up gun) before ever investigating the emotions the product evokes from customers.

Umpqua Bank

In comparison with the Google Glass example, Umpqua Bank took a very different approach. They innovated their entire business model from a human-centred perspective.

Umpqua are a small local bank franchise in Oregon, USA. Prior to the global financial crisis, they had a limited range of services to offer and a low community profile. In competition with major banks, Umpqua faced a critical question: 'Do we grow, or stagnate?' Engaging Ziba Design and using a design approach, Umpqua conceptualised financial services as products and took inspiration from retail franchises such as Starbucks. Their customer experience was to encapsulate five simple words: 'Surf. Sip. Read. Shop. Bank.' By working closely with their customers, Umpqua continually linked customers' businesses with other customers (for example, the local accountant who could assist doing the books of the local mechanic) to encourage shared wealth and community awareness and engagement. By selling services as products, and by providing a space in which to relax, socialise, shop and do financial things, Umpqua radically repositioned the business, using their customers as inspiration. When human-centred banking became the emotional cornerstone for the whole organisation, they made the following changes that all reinforced this agenda.

By asking local customers what they wanted and, more importantly, why they wanted it in their community, Umpqua developed a unique space for banking and community collaboration and integration. They discovered that their offerings were no different from those of their much larger competitors. They then identified local customers as the majority of their customer base. They discovered that customers were easily confused about different banking and financial offerings and services. Using the Starbucks experience, they asked how they could make Umpqua a destination where people want to be. How do we capture the broader community? What about selling financial services the same way as Starbucks sells coffee? They then converted the customer shops to provide a retail experience as a local community hub. All staff were educated on all aspects of the business; the bank manager was always around, and staff were integrated into the service offerings, recognising customers just like a Starbucks barista would.

Community integration was the key; they connected businesses in the community with other businesses to help them grow. The interior space of the shop was ahead of its time, with digital touchscreen displays for reading and a café inside the bank. There was even a surfboard rack at the door for the customers who had come straight from the surf. It turned into a community hub after hours, hosting local bands on Saturday nights and kids' events during the school holiday weekends (figure 4.2, overleaf). It was accessible and it engaged the community.

Figure 4.2: inspired by others: Umpqua makes banking personal

Creating and capturing value

A value proposition describes a company's current business purpose: a promise of value to be delivered, communicated and experienced by the customer. In previous times a value proposition was applied to different customer segments, products or services provided by an organisation. Today it is more commonly understood as the first step in a sustainable strategy. A value proposition is a statement of intended value, which should inform what digital stimulus is selected to reinforce the message of the value proposition (see figure 4.3.) For instance, Umpqua Bank's value proposition is community-centred banking.

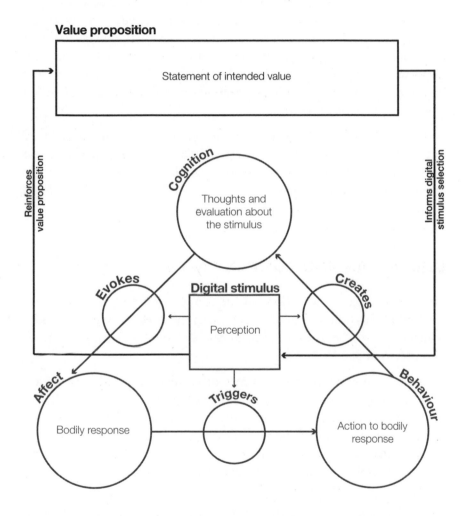

Figure 4.3: the position of a company's value proposition in the Affect Framework

Creating and delivering a value proposition is said to come from the inside out of an organisation. However, the principle of customer value, driving such decisions from the outside in, is easier said than done for most organisations. Contending with the ever-changing tides of emotional latent customer needs, institutions have to be agile in their strategic decisions. As a result, companies need to invest more resources into constantly monitoring customers' emotional needs and design/re-design their value propositions to suit these needs. The involvement of customers in co-designing a value proposition (from the outside in) is an important source of emotional insights that may have been overlooked by the company. So the following section explores what can be learned from the discipline of design.

Traditionally businesses employ design to create an artefact or outcome based on marketing research to enhance product development and sales. Only in recent history has design been used at an organisational level, designing experiences to foster positive emotional connections through understanding users and their interactions with a product or company.

UNDERSTANDING COMPANY AFFECT

There is a range of definitions of 'design', but for this book we have adopted Herbert Simon's general definition that 'design is the process by which we [derive] courses of action aimed at changing existing situations into preferred ones'.

Design can enhance the outcomes of business innovation activities, from the design of a product to its implementation strategies to a change in company culture. Internationally, governments have sponsored research into the contributions of design to a firm's performance and to the management of its creativity and design. An integrative design approach enables customers, employees and other stakeholders to co-create value.

If customers can align their values with that of an organisation, customer loyalty and employee motivation are dramatically improved. However, firms have difficulty providing the same clarity on the emotional (intangible) aspects of business activities as they do for functional requirements. Simon Sinek proposed in one of the most downloaded TED talks of all time that people don't buy what you do, but rather why you do it; this mantra has since given birth to the concept of the Golden Circles. Sinek's 'Golden Circle' has three layers:

1. why individuals are motivated to pursue goals

2. how the goals are achieved

3. what is the outcome of the process.

Sinek stresses that the 'why' question is the most important one; however, a majority of companies are primarily focused on communicating their 'what' (a description of product or service features). We believe that this can be overcome through the integration of design processes and philosophies. The design of a business strategy that creates the desired customer response to new products and services is as important to success as the products and services themselves. While designers have considered customer service and the role of emotion in products, the incorporation of emotion into the design of business innovation is not yet well understood. However, as customer emotions have a significant influence on purchase and consumption decisions, emotional needs are the foundation behind these decisions.

In order to hone a company's strategy to the desired affective state, we have to analyse the company's value proposition into a digital hedonic rhetoric code. This allows us to focus on what should be communicated and through what digital channel. Once you understand what emotion (affective state) you aim to evoke when a customer engages with your company, the right digital touchpoint can be designed.

DIGITAL HEDONIC RHETORIC

'Digital hedonic rhetoric' is the intended affect of the value proposition. It directs the message that should be communicated and reinforced through the selection of the digital stimulus. This can be seen in the context of the Affect Framework in figure 4.4 (overleaf).

A range of researchers have attempted to classify, define and measure emotions. For this book we are using Desmet's emotional typology to analyse the affective content of mission statements. The text was analysed in relation to a series of different emotions and their eliciting conditions, thus creating a multidimensional view of the emotional context of the text.

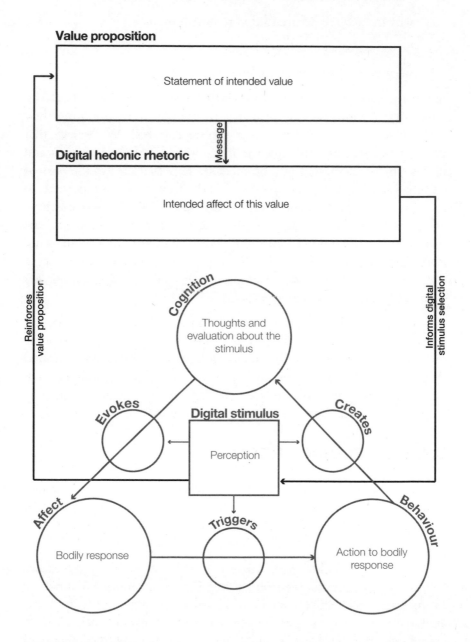

Figure 4.4: digital hedonic rhetoric: the intended affect of a company's value proposition

In table 4.1 nine of the 22 affective states and their eliciting conditions were used to analyse an organisation's intended message (digital hedonic rhetoric). This was due to the fact that negative affective states were deemed undesirable to most organisations. (What company wants to elicit a negative consumer response?)

Table 4.1: affective state classification

Affective state	Eliciting condition	Digital hedonic rhetoric examples
Pride	Approving of one's own praiseworthy action	To be the (most successful, provide the most compelling, safest, easiest)
		Leadership, legendary, world's leading provider, to champion, committed to
		Give customers what they want, to be the earth's most customer-centric company, to build a place, to enable, responsible, creative professionals, ensure fairness, integrity, passionate, unites, leading, delivering, best-run business, integrated systems
Hope	Fearing the worst but yearning for better	Improving the lives, vulnerable people, promotion, development, protects, basic human rights, harmony, future, conserving, diversity, ensuring, resources, sustainable, consumption, preventing, abuses, ending
Admiration	Approving of someone else's praiseworthy action	Pass on traditions, harmony in communities, people, planet, better everyday life for everyone, to be the standard by which others are measured, make aspirational quality, accessible
Desire	An object calls for possession or usage	Pleasure, superb, exclusive, high quality, effective, well-designed, functional, hot, celebrity inspired, fashionable, world's most valuable brand, move you with, enduring, natural

(continued)

Table 4.1: affective state classification (*cont'd*)

Affective state	Eliciting condition	Digital hedonic rhetoric examples
Stimulation	A promise for understanding through exploration or a new action	Creativity, exciting, earn trust, respect, integrity, reinvent, exceptional, experts, positive influence, want to help, revolutionise, enrich, creative, unique, time of their lives, spirited, inspire, curiosity, passion, connect, opportunities, supporting, build lifelong relationships, inspire awesomeness, improving lives, innovation, wellbeing, independence, care, brilliant, nothing is impossible, creative ideas, transform, transparent, enthusiastic, better future
Satisfaction	An expected goal realisation	Requirements met, highest quality manner, reliable, highest quality service, very best deal, delivering an experience, faster, exemplary customer service, excellence, enhancing, exceed expectations
Enjoyment	Liking a desirable or pleasant event	Creates joy, fun, affordable, environment, happiness
Pleasant surprise	An unexpected goal realisation	Well deserved, will exceed expectations, magical, fulfilled, enchanted, gratified
Love (liking)	Liking an appealing object	Deeply touched, feel warmth, feel deeply affectionate

Source: Synthesised from Desmet, 2005.

Analysis of a company's strategy into an affective state classification starts by asking qualitative questions: why do we do what we do? It targets communication in regard to human ideals (why), instead of business outcomes (what). By answering the 'why' questions, companies are able to uncover truths about their core values, leading to clarity, direction and alignment. Ignoring the affective or emotional content within texts may reduce the validity and ability to interpret the text. However, there are some difficulties in analysing the affective content of the text, many stemming from the fact that a significant number of emotions are not semantically distinct. But the affect eliciting conditions and the examples provided can be used to analyse a company's value proposition into digital hedonic rhetoric. Building upon the last example, Umpqua Bank's digital hedonic rhetoric was to build *pride* in the community, inclusivity of all customers regardless of *wealth*.

Kodak, as introduced in chapter 1, and their 'share memories, share life' motto failed to translate the basics of digital hedonic rhetoric into the channels that the customer cared about (as seen in figure 4.5, overleaf). They missed the market disruptor—Instagram. Failure to engage customers through communicating a company's value can result in under-performance, a loss of competitive advantage and missed business opportunities (as seen with Kodak).

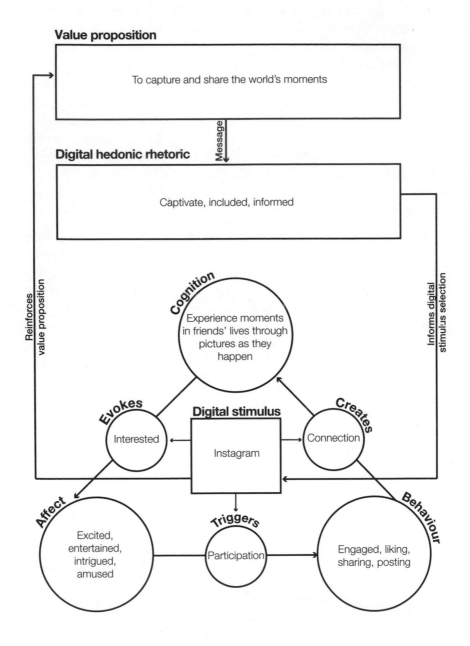

Figure 4.5: Instagram killed the Kodak star: Affect Framework

In order to explore this concept of digital hedonic rhetoric we studied 100 companies across 16 industries using the digital hedonic rhetoric index. This was to uncover the different underlying emotional drivers for different types of organisations. We found that 'pride' and 'stimulation' were common among all industries except non-profits and entertainment industries. Interestingly, non-profits were the only type of organisation to elicit pride and hope in their digital hedonic rhetoric, compared to the financial services sector, which elicited pride and satisfaction more prominently.

The results per industry are illustrated in figure 4.6.

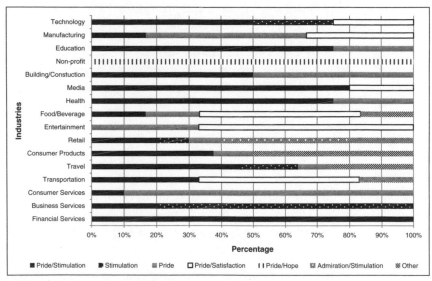

Figure 4.6: division of digital hedonic rhetoric per industry

The analysis of a company's value proposition into emotion-codes allows a focus on what should be communicated and through what digital channel. By understanding what emotion you aim to evoke when a customer engages with a company, the right digital touchpoint can be designed. Along with the channel typologies and touchpoints outlined and discussed in chapter 3, figure 4.6 provides a starting point for affect states based on industry classification.

CONFLICTING AFFECT MESSAGING

What do Lipton, Knorr, Dove, Omo and Lux have in common? They are all owned by Unilever. Unilever owns 400 brands, is based across five continents, and employs over 223 000 people separated into individual country teams who create their own brands, running their own marketing campaigns. But in 2000, with global competition becoming more intense, Unilever had to re-focus its core competencies and distil its efforts down to producing and marketing fast-moving consumer goods. The strategy was to create 'one Unilever' and unify all of its brands. The value proposition of the new strategy was, 'Add vitality to life. We meet everyday needs for nutrition, hygiene, and professional care with brands that help people feel good, look good and get more out of life'.

However, in 2004 Dove ran its 'Campaign for Real Beauty', which promoted healthy self-image for women, and was viewed over 7.4 million times on YouTube when it launched. Dove positioned itself in the market by encouraging women to love their bodies, with the aim of improving women's self-esteem. While this campaign was met with praise, it was also met with a lot of controversy. During this time, ads for Axe body spray (another Unilever brand) typically featured conventionally beautiful women who are seduced by men using Axe products. The depiction of women in these two campaigns sent conflicting messages. In addition to this Unilever also manufactures skin-lightening creams marketed in India and Slim-Fast, which seem to oppose the campaign for 'real beauty'.

Dove responded to the criticism by noting that advertising efforts 'are tailored to reflect the unique interests and needs of its audience'. However, we believe that Unilever as the parent company can and should find a way to advertise both products without contradicting the other. The framework in figure 4.7 shows how a consistent message can be held across the Unilever brands. Starting with the value proposition of the parent company (Unilever), the value propositions of the brands in the company can also be plotted (in this case Dove and Axe). The use of the affective state classification then should be used to choose words that can describe all three value propositions. From here the strategy can be created holistically, to align the message of each brand and avoid contradictions that could potentially damage customer engagement.

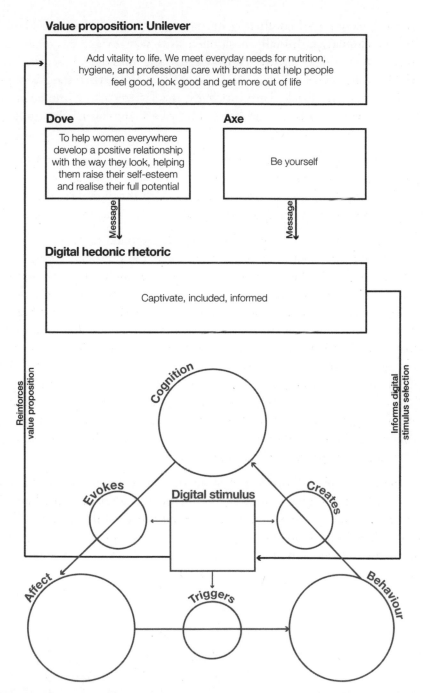

Figure 4.7: Unilever's mixed messages: the importance of knowing what is communicated

Another example of conflicting messaging is Aldi's 'fill in the blank' Twitter campaign. Initially positioned as a way to get customers to engage with the company, Aldi tweeted the message 'I became an ALDI lover when I tasted _____ for the first time', with the hashtags '#tellus' and '#feedback'. Unsurprisingly, the Twittersphere immediately answered with words such as 'horse', 'diarrhoea' and 'butts'. Australians are obviously very mature.

This response is a prime example of why companies need to approach their digital strategy holistically, not falling into the trap of making assumptions about how people will engage with the digital channel and, more importantly, if it aligns with the company's value proposition.

In 2014, Malaysia Airlines found itself embroiled in two passenger aircraft tragedies, with one plane disappearing and another being shot down, resulting in the loss of 537 lives. Unsurprisingly, due to these two events the airline took a financial hit, with the subsequent decline in ticket sales leading it to launch a promotional giveaway contest it hoped would reinvigorate the brand. The concept was simple—submit your dream holiday destination for a chance to win a plane ticket there—but the name of the contest—My Ultimate Bucket List—was not. The public were horrified that the airline's contest was labelled as fulfilling a 'bucket list'—a list of things people hope to do before they die—when considering the hundreds of passengers in 2014 who had died flying Malaysian Airlines. The airline issued an apology and removed any reference to the promotion's original title.

These examples illustrate the strategic implications for misaligned and conflicting digital channels. A holistic and aligned multichannel strategy is vital, but so is sticking to it. A very successful example of this is described in the following case study on Burberry Love. After that, it's on to Part III, which is all about strategy.

Falling in Burberry Love

Luxury brand managers in particular should focus on experiential marketing by taking the essence of a product and translating it into a set of experiences that amplify the brand. Burberry ranked ninety-fourth on *Forbes'* list of the world's most valuable brands and eighth on the Luxury Institute of New York list at the time of writing. Known worldwide for their distinctive tartan pattern, Burberry distributes clothing and fashion accessories, and also licenses fragrances. We have selected them for this section due to their digital channel strategy of building the digital hedonic rhetoric 'Burberry Love' theme, becoming a market leader in digital communications within the competitive sector of luxury brands. The luxury goods market has become increasingly complex, as it requires an image of quality, performance and authenticity, but also an experience by relating it to the lifestyle of its consumers. To understand Burberry's strategy, we explored the digital channels and customer responses in relation to five Burberry digital campaigns.

THE DIGITAL CHALLENGE IN LUXURY FASHION

In a society that offers an abundance of choices of products and services from a number of companies, forming relationships with customers is critical for customer retention. The challenges of integrating luxury branding on the internet and in digital environments are due to the common belief that luxury is a product, an object, a service or a lifestyle, when in fact it is an identity, a philosophy and a culture.

In translating into a digital environment, you need to associate with what constructs the brand as luxury, evoking exclusivity. If you have a well-known brand identity, enjoy high brand awareness and perceived quality, there is the opportunity to retain sales levels and customer loyalty. The luxury fashion sector is unique in that its customers acquire goods for what they symbolise and represent. Contemporary customers use these goods to make statements about themselves, to create identities and develop a sense of belonging. These customers have formed a new individualistic consumption model, driven by new needs and a desire for experiences.

Even though the internet and digital channels play a significant role in fuelling the universal appeal of luxury brands, to a global consumer group there is a perception that digital channels have a negative impact on the innate attributes of luxury brands such as 'prestige' and 'exclusivity'. Luxury brands are concerned that misrepresentation in digital translation can lead to losing the aura of the brand. However, the successful implementation and management of digital channels is necessary to maintain and sustain a competitive advantage in this particular industry sector. Consumers of luxury goods are among the global consumer population that crave continuous internet access. The luxury-purchase decision process uses a high dose of emotions and irrationality, which are boosted by a high-impact experience. Therefore, emotional engagement of online customers throughout the company's digital channels is particularly necessary for luxury brands.

The retail environment is becoming more competitive than ever, with e-commerce growing significantly, outpacing traditional retail channels. The fashion industry is slower than other sectors to adopt technology. One main reason for this is the difficulty of translating the in-store experience to the online environment. Clothing is considered to be a high-involvement product category, related to personal identity and products that need to be seen, touched and tried on because they are difficult to evaluate in a virtual environment. However, technology has enabled shopping online to become interactive and exciting, which has led us to explore how emotions can build digital channel relationships with customers.

BUSINESS CASE: BURBERRY

Burberry have a rich history. At over 150 years old, their fashion has seen the trenches of World War I, and they have been an official supplier to the royal family and been worn by a range of celebrities. Burberry were known as British fashion royalty, however, over time this reputation deteriorated and they seemed to have lost their competitive advantage among the global luxury brands. Burberry therefore changed their vision in 2006, to be 'the first company who is fully digital' and 'to build a social enterprise'. This vision was formed after a loss of net profits, the expansion of their fashion and beauty lines, and an incoherent marketing strategy globally. The aim of this new vision was to provide an experience for customers to access 'Burberry across all devices, anywhere, anytime' with the same consistent brand image. The driving business model was 'a distinctive global luxury brand'.

The aim of their strategy was to 'speak to consumers with one equally authentic and inspiring brand voice, whenever they encounter the brand'. To engage consumers with the brand, Burberry developed increasingly personalised and connected experiences across all digital touchpoints.

With this new vision, came a new target audience, Millennials (born between 1980 and 2000). With this new target audience, who were overlooked by other luxury brands, Burberry had to rethink their entire marketing approach. Their response was to make it digital, starting with their website, which was redesigned to have 'everything in one place' to showcase every facet of the brand, become the hub of all marketing and branding, and highlight the Burberry trench coat. The website was also designed to speak to the Millennial customer through 'emotive brand content: music, movies, heritage, storytelling'. The digital channel makes the brand accessible to a wider audience, from 'brand browsers' to 'brand advocates'. The 'Burberry Love' theme has been successful in motivating its target audience to engage in and share the experience with others. This behaviour is evident through the growth impact (brand and revenue) and high level of customer engagement with each channel.

Burberry's digital channel presence includes over 16 million followers on Facebook, over 3 million on Twitter and over 2 million on Instagram. This increase in online consumer commitment also resulted in an increase in gross revenue. Figure F illustrates this growth in revenue over a ten-year period (2004 to 2014) and its relationship to the launch of five digital campaigns. It can be inferred that the new direction in 2006 and development of digital channels since 2009 has created a substantial growth in revenue.

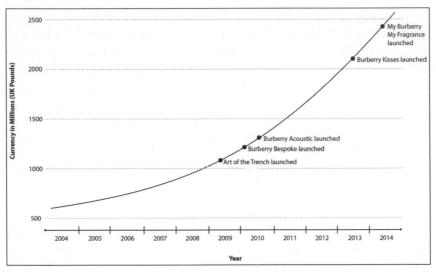

Figure F: growth over 10 years from annual reports 2006–14 in UK pounds

THE FIVE DIGITAL CAMPAIGNS

Burberry's strategy involved five different digital campaigns.

My Burberry My Fragrance

Launched: December 2014

Touchpoints: personalised TV commercial, interactive billboard, Twitter, Facebook, Pinterest, Google+, Burberry website

The interactive digital campaign (see figure G) invited customers via TV ads, billboards and social media ads to have their initials carved on a bottle of new fragrance, My Burberry, for free, using the brand's monogramming service. They would then purchase the bottle online at burberry.com, and live mapping directions would guide them to the nearest Burberry store where they could collect their monogrammed My Burberry bottle. Users could also share their bespoke bottle across social media platforms.

Figure G: My Burberry My Fragrance

Burberry Kisses

Launched: June 2013

Touchpoints: Burberry website, Google Maps, YouTube

Burberry collaborated with Google to re-imagine how brands can deliver beautiful, emotional experiences across devices and screens (see figure H). The idea was to send messages sealed with your real kiss. Facial recognition technology detected the outline of a user's lips through their webcam. To add a further personal touch to every letter sent, they used location data. For example, as users saw their messages travel to their destination across a 3D landscape, they could see local landmarks and Street View images reflected into puddles, further bringing the experience to life.

Figure H: Burberry Kisses

Burberry Acoustic

Launched: 2010

Touchpoints: Burberry website, YouTube

Burberry Acoustic was a website that streamed to Burberry stores around the world (see figure I). It was a reflection of Burberry's authentic dedication to giving young British bands an opportunity to break through (while wearing Burberry clothing), using all its multimedia platforms. Florence and the Machine, Coco Sumner, Life in Film, The Kooks and One Night Only were all featured.

Figure I: Burberry Acoustic

Burberry Bespoke

Launched: 2010

Touchpoints: Burberry website

Burberry Bespoke (see figure J) allowed customers to design their own customised coat by choosing from hundreds of different options, from the buttons on the outside to the lining in the inside, and even a personalised monogram option. Customers could buy it online, request an appointment, live chat with customer service or share their design across social media.

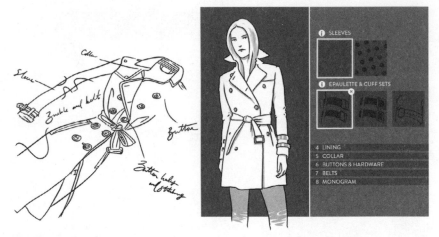

Figure J: Burberry Bespoke

The Art of the Trench

Launched: October 2009

Touchpoints: Instagram, Pinterest, Burberry website

Burberry's the Art of the Trench (see figure K) was described as 'a living celebration of the Burberry trench coat and the people who wear it'. The website, Instagram and Pinterest page featured photos of men and women dressed in the classic trench coat. The photos came from user-submitted images posted on Instagram or Pinterest. Users got to see hundreds of different people wearing the coat while listening to a soundtrack of up-and-coming artists. There was also an option to filter the style of trench by colour, style and gender. Burberry selected their favourite submitted images and posted them on the main site.

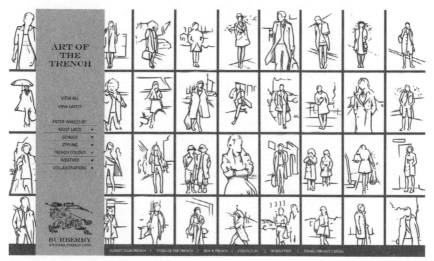

Figure K: Art of the Trench

ANALYSING BURBERRY'S SUCCESS

We collected relevant information for each digital campaign from secondary sources. In an ideal world we would have loved to be on the inside of Burberry while all this was unfolding, as we were with the case study of Cj Hendry, however in this case we began with a search of the company's website, and from there analysed documentation such as annual reports and other publicly available reports. Five different types of data were collected from secondary sources in order to validate the results from multiple perspectives.

After the content of the five Burberry campaigns were analysed. Two key emotional drivers were identified. These were stimulation (a promise for understanding through exploration or a new action) and pride (approving of one's own praiseworthy action).

For each campaign, key digital touchpoints included the Burberry website and social touchpoints Facebook, Instagram, Pinterest and YouTube to engage customers. The content on these touchpoints is primarily for promotion (to attract customers), with the purpose of diversion (for customers to participate in recreational and social activities through the channel) and interaction (two-way communication with the company or a community of customers). We selected customer comments from these digital touchpoints and were analysed, resulting in six emotions (satisfaction, desire, admiration, enjoyment, stimulation and love). We then linked these emotions to Burberry's value proposition and core strategies. We also included the impacts of the campaigns to illustrate the success and reach of each. Details and lessons from the Burberry Love campaign are explored in the next section and explained through the Digital Affect Framework (figure L).

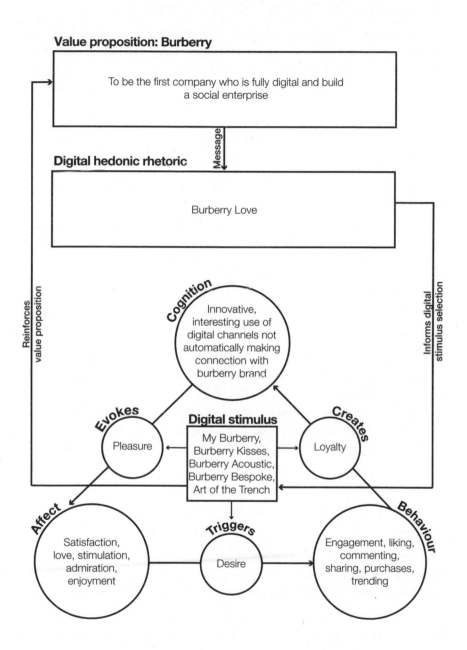

Figure L: Burberry Digital Affect Framework

Company and customer engagement

Associated: Feelings, Emotions, Moods and Experiences

Customer needs determine the type of interaction they desire. Creating an emotional experience is complex and involves many differing factors. However, it is affect (feelings, emotions and moods) that will have the greatest influence. Customers will have associated feelings, emotions, moods and past experiences with a company. Associations could be linked to branding, advertising or social interactions with the company. In order to provide customers with experiences, the underlining emotions must first be understood in considerable depth.

First we must understand the customers' needs and desires, and then we design an experience that best meets those needs. Burberry observed their target customer and realised that Millennials are more influenced by peers than by anything that a brand may have to say. Insight into customer emotions and behaviour is imperative in the luxury sector, as the luxury customer is individualistic and knows what they want and how they prefer to interpret their personal style. They therefore want to stamp their personality on a luxury brand and use products and fashion as a reflection of their identity, doing so in their way and on their own terms, while highlighting the 'luxury' prestige status.

Through evoking key emotions such as desire and stimulation, Burberry's touchpoints, such as Burberry Bespoke and the Art of the Trench, turn this interaction into a social activity. Customers invest time into either designing their own Burberry trench coat or photographing themselves wearing it.

Designing digital channels

Evoking: Feelings, Emotions and Moods that align with the brand and customer

The emotional association with the company will evoke an affective response. Digital channels need to be designed to evoke positive responses, satisfaction and pleasurable experiences over a period of time.

All Burberry's digital channels are driven by promotional content, to evoke the theme of 'Burberry Love'. This is created by the range of Burberry-composed stories expressed across the digital channels and through products, events, social media and PR.

Good digital channel design can enhance customer experiences by emphasising and accentuating the brand characteristics. Burberry's digital channels are not driven by revenue; the main objective is to connect people through the Burberry brand. Through these channels, Burberry creates their own community inspired by their core product: the trench coat. The design of the channels also allows for personalisation and customisation of products and services, which contributes to customer emotions such as enjoyment, stimulation and satisfaction, leading to brand loyalty and enhanced relationships. All channels create and share content among Burberry communities, generating online brand circulation. All these individual components add to the overall strategy of inviting others to be part of the Burberry story.

Digital customer experience

Creating: Attitude, Behaviour and Meaning

The emotions evoked through the digital channel create an attitude, behaviour and meaning for the brand. Over time this will form positive emotional connections with the experience and company. Memorable positive experiences lead to positive behaviours towards the company and, in turn, form loyal customers.

Burberry's digital channels evoke positive emotions usually associated with being in love, which is a strong emotion for motivating certain behaviours. Love as an emotion is seemingly irrational, and the behaviour outcomes of being in love could lead to customers seeing money as no object in achieving their desired feelings.

Through the five different channels, customers are brought together to be part of the Burberry story. Music, kisses and customising are free of charge and help build goodwill for a loyal customer. Engagement with all digital channels results in customer behaviours of 'liking', commenting, personalising, purchasing or sharing the experience with others. This approach can only make more potential customers aware of the brand, as current customers and advocates help sell it.

* * *

Through all Burberry's digital campaigns, their customers are motivated by a set of key emotions, resulting in them being 'part of the Burberry story'. Each digital channel provides a unique yet consistent message, bringing together the brand, culture and customers in the same story. This story aligns with the brand DNA (British heritage) and the key product (trench coat).

Emotions play a large part in luxury goods, with customers developing an emotional affair with luxury brands, instead of one driven by cognition. Burberry play on this concept of the 'emotional affair' by building a relationship through the digital channels, allowing customers to participate in the experience and then communicate this with others.

The Burberry channels outlined also match the digital knowledge and daily habits of their Millennial target customer. Millennials currently use most of the digital channels in their daily lives, so engagement via these channels is easy and intuitive. The range of different interactions across the Burberry digital channels allows the user to borrow the Burberry brand to reflect their own identities, representing someone with great, high-end fashion sense.

This is the other key strategy of all of Burberry's digital channels: 'personalisation' via the 'Burberry Love' theme. From personalising the perfume bottle to customisation of the classic Burberry coat, this individual tailoring has been proven to strengthen the connection between users and a product, as possessions can symbolically define and express identity (as discussed in chapter 2). By injecting meaning into products consumers own and view as valuable, they are able to display a piece of themselves through that product, reinforcing the 'sense of self'.

Strong emotions, memories and enjoyment during use can also contribute to the level of attachment an individual feels towards a certain object, so creating an emotional bond between consumer and product can lead to increased levels of attachment and loyalty. Through sharing content such as 'selfies' of their customised coats and ownership of their perfume bottle, their identity is connected to that of the Burberry brand.

IMPACT AND CHALLENGES OF EMOTION-DRIVEN DIGITAL INNOVATION

This study illustrates the impact of digital channel engagement. Falling in 'love' with the Burberry brand is aided through the emotions evoked and connections formed throughout the experiences on the digital channels. Failure to engage customers emotionally may result in underperformance, loss of competitive advantage and missed opportunities. Designing, managing and continually evolving a customer's emotional experience is incredibly complex due to the varying expectations, messages and values of the customer, company and digital channels. Financial and competitive advantages in this case resulted due to the higher user involvement with the digital channel (e.g. time spent, number of pages viewed, amount of personal information revealed), translating into revenue.

Customer perceptions of the investment made by a company in the interactivity of digital channels can have an impact on the quality of the relationship and the their willingness to provide and share positive company experiences with others. Customer engagement via digital channels requires a combination of creativity, deep emotional understanding, knowledge of digital behaviour and a strong company-to-customer strategy that has the full picture mapped out. This involves including customer motivations and requirements, all guided by a strong company-to-customer emotional strategy for initiating relationships.

Key lessons from Burberry Love

- Start with understanding your customer and how they interact in the digital world.

- Understand *why* they engage in the digital world.

- Interact with them in their world, how they want to be connected with.

- Discover their daily habits and behaviours.

- Base your digital strategy upon these behaviours.

- Select your digital channels to best match these behaviours.

- Build an affective brand through experiences as well as branding.

- Don't jump into connecting digital engagements with your brand.

- Different digital campaigns should be designed together, even if executed separately or not at the same time or on different channel platforms.

- Design the digital channel to bridge the physical and virtual experience (and in some cases bridge different digital platforms) through the same emotion and seamless experience.

- Push technological boundaries—do something unique with the channel's existing technology.

- Know when to be bold with engagements and when to be more subtle.

PART III

Affective strategy

CHAPTER 5

Designing affect: The Digital Affect Framework

Customers are better informed than ever before—expectations are high and loyalty is rare. How customers feel about a product, service or business can drastically alter their engagement with and behaviour toward a company and influence the likelihood of them being loyal.

This rapidly evolving landscape has left leaders at a loss, and what we are experiencing is likely the beginning of a tectonic shift in the way digital channels are designed, monitored and managed. Companies need new forms of knowledge and processes that allow them to create lasting engagements with their customers.

In this chapter, we present useful concepts for clarifying and refining the emotional meaning behind an organisation's strategy, and its relationship to corresponding digital channels. Through examples we discuss the process and impact of 'emotionally aware' digital channel designs. We also make recommendations on how to select, design and maintain digital engagements based on your strategy as well as industry needs.

LOYALTY IS A RARITY

Consumers are no longer loyal. However, some customers may be loyal to the engagement experience (digital stimulus) that one particular brand offers over another. Consumers gravitate toward experiences that provide them with the emotional engagement they are searching for. Once the experiential elements of the engagement disappear, in many cases so does the emotional connection consumers have with the company that was providing them.

We have less recreational time than ever before, so naturally we are guarded about how we spend it and what inspires us to do so. If a company focuses on trying to sell consumers their products or services rather than finding creative ways to engage with them through their down time, their brand will be short-lived.

Speaking of cultivating loyalty, Kmart managed to do exactly this in a marketplace full of tight retail competition. In Australia only eight years ago it was difficult to imagine that Kmart could or would ever be classified as stylish, modern or trendy—and yet currently they are being admired as just that. Back in 2008 Kmart were lagging behind more profitable rivals such as Big W and Target and, although the retail giant had a turnover of AU$4 billion a year, zero of it was profit. They sat close to bankruptcy for years, until finally a new chief executive was brought in to resuscitate the organisation. Over the span of six years they went from zero profit to AU$289 million earnings before interest and taxes at the close of 2014. Since then, Kmart have gone from strength, to strength posting even greater profits more recently, and they have avoided bankruptcy, becoming the most profitable retailer in Australia.

The company had many issues prior, including a bloated business model with no concise strategy, an overpopulated product stock list and confusing pricing structures. The rebranding Kmart underwent was not superficial; it was a complete strategic transformation. Kmart unreservedly embraced change to become Australia's top homeware and fashion retailer, and they did so with the captivating recipe of on-trend products at simple low prices.

Recent times have seen the brand enjoy considerable social media attention, and astonishingly, most of it is organic. With thousands of Australian customers following countless unofficial Kmart fan accounts and sharing their purchases and personal style, the 'Cult of Kmart' has dominated Facebook and Instagram. Hashtags such as #kmarthack, #kmartstyling, #kmartaddictsunite and #kmartswag have an enthusiastic online following, instantaneously creating a bonded community and establishing Kmart as an aspirational brand (for more on the community digital channel typology, see chapter 3).

The idea behind the 'Kmart hack' (see figure 5.1) is to first purchase items from Kmart, and then to re-create different products by painting, gluing and all-round re-purposing (as demonstrated by using a basket for a coffee table) afterwards and then posting it online and sharing it with the Kmart hacker community. There are a number of social media pages devoted to these hacks, and large numbers of Australian customers that share their own hacks and DIY makeovers utilising Kmart products.

Figure 5.1: cultivating community: Kmart hacks

Thousands of penny-saving mums are posting images of their purchases (before and after 'hack' shots), tagging their wish lists and sharing mood boards of products and home décor advice. The growth in popularity has been organic and not coordinated by head office, with customers creating their own vast communities to immediately share their opinions and like other members' creations. In this case it worked in Kmart's favour, but as you will see in other examples shortly, this does not always yield positive results for the company.

DECONSTRUCTING THE DIGITAL AFFECT FRAMEWORK

As discussed throughout this book, the process of creating an emotional experience is complex and involves many different factors. Emotions are functional because they pull us *towards* certain people, objects, actions and ideas, and push us *away* from others. Pleasant emotions pull us to products that are (or promise to be) constructive, whereas unpleasant emotions will push us from those that are (or promise to be) detrimental to our wellbeing. Customer loyalty can only be developed if a company can build emotional connections in addition to positive attitudes and behaviours. Positive memorable experiences with a company are key to creating emotionally loyal customers.

Traditional market research cannot anticipate quick shifts in customer preferences, tastes, habits and lifestyles, so companies need to be engaged with their customers on a deeper level to understand not *what* they want but *why* they want it.

The field of design and emotion has various tools and methods for understanding customers' needs, aspirations and feelings through predominantly asking 'why' questions. This empathic approach places emphasis on understanding the emotional aspects of a customer–product or customer–company relationship. Companies should be delving deeper by questioning customers and inviting them to interact, rather than simply reacting to questions and instructions. By replacing the passive view of a customer with an active one, organisations can gain new insights and opportunities to design interactive and valuable digital channel engagements. See the Burberry case study for a great example of this kind of engagement.

The Digital Affect Framework (see figure 5.2) collectively brings together the elements explored in the previous chapters. When used holistically it outlines the steps required for an organisation to become emotionally aware and inform its strategy with a deeper understanding of its customers.

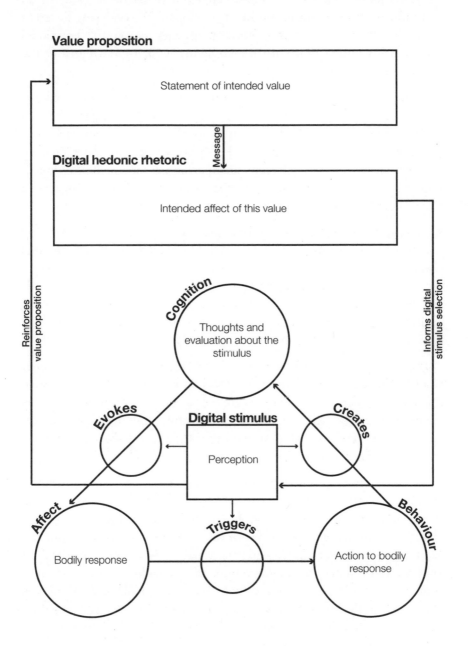

Figure 5.2: Digital Affect Framework

The Digital Affect Framework illustrates that cognition (what we think), emotion (what we feel) and behaviour (what we do) are related and influence each other (as outlined in chapter 2). Analysing different customer affective states is important, as they create the emotional experience of interaction with the company, which contributes to the meaning and emotional response.

Inputs such as a company's value proposition and the digital hedonic rhetoric (outlined in chapter 4) create perceptions of the company through the messages and the digital stimulus (outlined in chapter 3) it puts out. These two parts (the inputs and outputs) are key in understanding the relationship formed between customer and company. Not only is it important for future planning, but it is required for determining how a strong relationship can be built over time.

A company must plan its digital channel strategy by first understanding the critical, important and impartial requirements of digital channel usage. This stage of planning requires exploring the company's current use of digital touchpoints and what the industry digital channel standards and requirements are. This understanding is important in designing digital channels because it helps ensure that customer needs will be met through the digital engagement.

By starting with people, companies can uncover individual customer emotional needs, and in turn understand how to design for their needs. Putting customer emotions at the centre of a company's business strategy strengthens relationships, providing innovative digital channel design opportunities. It is important to note that the process should start with the customer and not an existing solution or digital channel.

This chapter is approaching the same end state, but from an organisation's point of view so that the two (the organisation and the customer) align simultaneously through their values and convert into an emotional experience. From this, organisations can design the right digital channel strategy for their needs by understanding their own affective state, the requirements of the industry and customer content needs. It is through values that individuals feel connected and emotionally committed to a company, so it is essential that values match. As value gives meaning, and meaning is heavily intertwined with emotion.

This framework is presented in appendix B in a template format to encourage you to experiment. The following sections outline the three components of the framework:

1. understanding your industry

2. understanding your customer

3. understanding your digital engagements.

Value proposition: Understanding your industry

Deciphering a company's value internally can be more difficult for some than others, as this may not be known across all areas of a company or indeed within the management team (as some of our industry projects have shown). Therefore, it may require work to first get to the core value of why the business exists in the first place. Who do they serve? An analysis of the company strategy may be required to get to the emotional drivers. Once the company value is known, it can be converted into an emotional experience for the customer. The desired affective state and the eliciting condition (digital hedonic rhetoric) underpin the meaning behind the company's strategy, and they should align with how the company wants their customers to feel every time they engage with them. This is discussed in chapters 2 and 4.

It is important for organisations to also continually look outward at the industry as a whole, to gain insights into changes from potential disruptors (such as Airbnb to the hotel industry and Uber to the taxi industry) and also for new perspectives, such as Cj Hendry seeing art as a potentially profitable business. Is the value for an industry in a state of change? For example airports, traditionally designed to service airlines, becoming a hub for passengers' travel experiences, and a destination in themselves.

Key questions to ask to understand your company's value and the state of play of the industry include:

• What is the current state of business models in the industry?

• Where is the industry heading? Are there any potential disruptors?

- What is the value that other companies offer in your industry? Are they all similar?

- Do you think their value offering is going to change?

- What is your value offering? Is this the same as others in your industry?

- How is your value communicated to your customers?

- Do you think your customer aligns with your values?

Value proposition checklist:

- Make sure everyone in the company understands and knows the value offering.

- Don't conflict with any parent or partner company's values.

- Redesign the company's value if it's no longer relevant.

Digital hedonic rhetoric: Understanding your customer

Digital hedonic rhetoric starts and ends with understanding your customers and how they interact in the digital world. This process aims to create an understanding of why customers engage in the digital world, to inform how you should interact with them in their world. This requires knowing what their daily habits and behaviours are, and building your digital strategy upon these behaviours. You may be looking at the wrong problems or issues; start by asking your customers what they believe be their biggest problems are.

In order to provide customers with positive experiences, the underlying meaning of these experiences must be understood in considerable depth. Customer meaning is explored in the same way a company's is: through identifying desired affective states and their eliciting conditions. The interaction between a company and customer is a blend of the company's physical performance, the associations it stimulates and the emotions it evokes, measured against the customer's expectations across all moments of contact. A customer's expectations are essential, so it is necessary to first understand their associated feelings, emotions, moods and experiences in relation to the company.

Customer needs relate to the type of interaction the customer wants. What feelings, emotions and moods are evoked through their interaction with a company? Digital channels should be designed to evoke positive responses, satisfaction and pleasurable experiences over a period of time.

To gain this understanding, we need to gather data relating to:

- the individual customer
- their current awareness and use of company digital channels
- the emotions being experienced by the customer when interacting with the company and the reasons behind these emotions.

The main intent of this is to decipher why customers experience certain emotions, and to establish a link between the experience (attributes), their response (consequences) and related personal values.

Digital channels must be well publicised and perceived as useful and user-friendly by customers, otherwise they are unlikely to use them. Customers who are aware of available digital channels have a higher rate of pleasant experiences. Our research has indicated that perceived usability, loyalty, trust and satisfaction are interrelated, as these indicators increased when a customer's expectations of the system were confirmed.

Key questions to ask to understand your customer include:

- Who is your customer?
- Should they be your customer?
- What do they value?
- What are their perceptions of the company?
- Do your customer's values align with what you are offering?
- Why does the customer value this?

Digital hedonic rhetoric checklist:

- Have a conversation with your customers. Don't simply ask if they like or dislike something; ask them what they value and why.

Digital stimulus: Understanding your digital engagements

Digital stimulus is more than just posting content on a channel; it is a way to communicate your company's value and provide memorable experiences. This should start with designing an experience that you want your customer to have with your company. Once you identify your desired experience and emotions, this can help you select the right channels or, if they don't yet exist, design a new one. Design the digital channel to bridge the gap between the digital and physical experience with the company or products (or in some cases bridge back to other digital channels), however always keep in mind that the emotions evoked should align with the core values, providing a seamless experience. (This also involves understanding when to be bold with engagements and when to be subtle. For example, when customers only require basic information, a functional channel is usually the best solution.) Consistency of messages should expand to all aspects of the company, including campaigns, ensuring that they are designed together even if executed separately or over a number of channels.

The quality of an interaction with a company via its digital channels will have an impact on customers' behaviour and motivations to engage with the company again. Memorable positive experiences lead to positive behaviours and loyalty towards the company.

In the concept of 'progression of economic value', experiences are a new economic offering (after commodities, goods and services).[2] Experiences are a new lever for providing value to both the company and the customer. From this perspective, companies do not sell experiences, but rather they provide products and contexts that can be employed by customers to co-create their own unique experiences. Customer experience is made up of physical and emotional elements and is not about the delivery of the product or service, but how it made them feel.

Emotions affect attitudes and behaviours towards companies, as well as the economic value of long-term customer relationships. Positive experiences result in comfortable and relaxed customers, which in turn leads to repeat business, higher spending rates and ultimately increased revenues. Therefore, providing customers with pleasant experiences through the awareness and use of digital channels is paramount. And keep in mind: it is not only about the channel but about how people use it — and if they will use it at all!

Key questions to ask to understand your digital engagements include:

- What channels does the industry traditionally currently use?
- Are customers engaging with these channels? If so, how are they engaging?
- What are they saying?

- What is the purpose of your existing channels?

- Do your current digital channels match the needs of your customers?

- What value does the channel bring the user and the company?

Digital stimulus checklist:

- Decide on a distinct visceral aesthetic style that represents the value proposition and branding.

- If the perfect channel doesn't exist, make your own.

- Push technological boundaries — do something unique with the existing technology of the channel.

- Benchmark other digital strategies and channels in the same industries.

- Look to other industries to inspire your digital channel selection and experience.

Think before you post

Once you understand your value proposition, digital hedonic rhetoric and digital stimulus and start to craft your approach, keep this checklist in mind before posting:

- Remember the message to your customers about the company's value.

- What have your previous messages said about your company?

- Have a deliberate plan: understand the emotion you want to elicit.

- What emotion will this elicit? Is it aligned with the value proposition?

- How does what I'm stating in this post reinforce the emotion/ digital hedonic rhetoric of the company?

- Does it match the style of the channel?

- Does it play to the strengths of that channel? (e.g. pictures for Instagram)

- Do the images and text align?

- Understand the use of text, such as hashtags, remembering consistency and nuances, and potential misunderstandings.

- Does it align with the visceral aesthetic style of the brand?

EXAMPLES OF ALIGNING VALUES TO EXPERIENCES

As stated before, in order to provide customers with experiences, the underlying emotions they have about the company must first be understood. An emotional commitment develops when the customer identifies with the values of a company and the emotional drivers behind its strategy. The importance of a sense of meaning is heavily explored in the field of design and emotion, as the customer mindset is a key driver of company performance.

However, with the growing number of channels, companies are faced with the challenge of unifying their online value across multiple channels and engaging with customers in a way that is not only consistent and true to their company value, but also that engages customers in their sense of meaning. Since customers can engage and share their own content, they are empowered to express and publish positive and negative experiences with or without the company's permission, so mistakes can have a huge impact on a company's reputation. On the other hand, these new digital channels combined with increasing levels of digital literacy also allow organisations to embed customers as co-designers and co-producers of company value and meaning, like in the Kmart example earlier in this chapter.

As initially discussed in chapter 1, the digital Kate Spade storefront, which integrates online shopping with a real-world environment, aims to evoke desired emotions that reflect the brand's identity and their 'Saturday Girl' (figure 5.3), their ideal customer. When designing this digital engagement, they understood the negatives to purchasing clothing online, such as not knowing the right size and the item not arriving on time. To create a positive experience, multiple sizes can be ordered, as a Kate Spade courier politely waits for the customer to try on multiple sizes and only takes payment on the items the customer wishes to purchase.

Figure 5.3: Kate Spade: overcoming the negatives of online shopping

Through the use of mobile technology, they were able to use the benefits of digital shopping (such as 24-hour access) and place it into the physical world. The use of technology here is to make the storefront less about selling and more about creating an experience, giving shoppers a reason to engage with the company. See figure 5.4 for the Digital Affect Framework of Kate Spade's 'Saturday Girl'.

As discussed in chapter 1, Meat Pack's 'Hijack' campaign 'stole' customers from their competitors (see figure 5.5, overleaf).

Figure 5.4: changing behaviours: Meat Pack's Hijack

The experience of using the mobile application was undoubtedly fun and memorable and more effective than a traditional discount voucher, resulting in a significant behaviour change (running from a competitor's store). The long-term effects on behaviour are seen in the engagement via other digital channels such as Facebook, which have helped promote the store through positive engagements. See figure 5.6 (overleaf) for the Digital Affect Framework for Hijack.

This, along with Kmart's authentic community of followers who take it upon themselves to promote and share in their online community, is the stuff that social media managers dream of. See figure 5.7 (see p146) for the Digital Affect Framework for Kmart's 'hacks'.

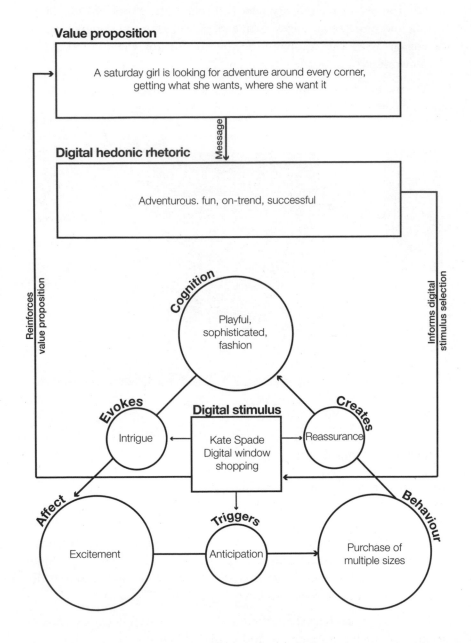

Figure 5.5: Kate Spade's 'Saturday Girl' Framework

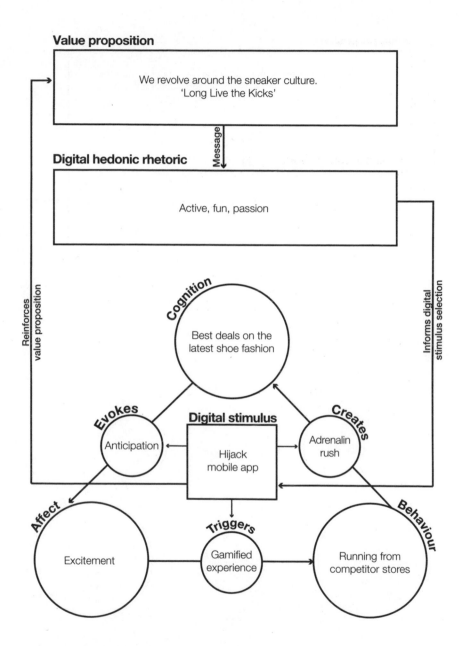

Figure 5.6: Hijack Digital Affective Framework

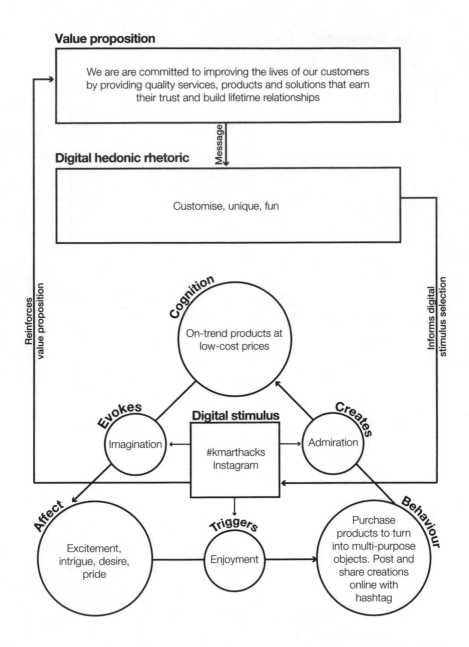

Figure 5.7: Kmart Hack Affective Framework

US-based company American Apparel provides us with an example of the huge impact a mistake can have. Three decades ago in 1986, the tragic explosion of the space shuttle Challenger (which killed all seven astronauts on board) just 73 seconds after lift-off provided one of the most distressing images of the late twentieth century. Fast forward to 2014. This image was used by American Apparel—for their Fourth of July festivities. American Apparel's social media team uploaded the image of the disintegrating shuttle to the brand's Tumblr blog, tagging the image 'smoke' and 'clouds'. As outraged customers and members of the public reacted all over social media the company quickly apologised and took the image down. 'We deeply apologize for today's Tumblr post ... The image was re-blogged in error by one of our international social media employees who was born after the tragedy and was unaware of the event', the company said on Twitter. However, the apology did not stop the viral spread of disdain for the company. This highly visible customer relationship is created online and can, as this example shows, be nearly impossible to reverse once the damage is done.

AFFECTED PRINCIPLES

For companies to build awareness of different innovation strategies, tools and processes, as well as adopt and embed these approaches within their organisation, it requires not only a strong Fox manager but also Foxes at all levels of the business. This demands not only strong leadership but also an inquisitive company culture, allowing for the participation of customers in co-creating brand identity. Companies can strategically use this involvement to inform and strengthen their relationships with customers.

This chapter has demonstrated that in order to execute an affected strategy, it will need to be bigger than the design of one digital channel. It goes back to the roots of your company and the strategic values it holds. By understanding and agreeing on this, the rest of the Digital Affect Framework can be designed and implemented successfully. To ensure the alignment of values to experience, we have created the following 'principles of affect', which should be used to guide all digital engagements with customers. They are as follows:

- Like all great design, less is more.
- If you created it, you need to maintain it.
- Don't follow the trend.
- Alignment is crucial.
- Your customers are your greatest asset.
- We might not remember the details, but we will remember how it made us feel.

These are to be used in conjunction with the Digital Affect Framework seen in Appendix B.

Like all great design, less is more.

Remember it is better to have fewer channels that provide true value to your customers than to have many channels that are inactive. Likewise, it is better to have a small amount of well-designed content on some channels than to have masses of posts that mean nothing. You also have to respond to and engage with the audience of your channel and the content that you provide in it. Take your time and craft something meaningful . Quality over quantity is always the key.

Don't forget: Be considered and consistent.

If you created it, you need to maintain it.

There is nothing worse than searching for a company and clicking on a social media site only to find out that it has been inactive for months or even years. Remember the Heinz sauce bottle example and the German porn site? Maintain your domain hosting! Consider that all representations of the company will influence a customer's perspective and have an impact on their experience. If you are smart about it, you can even leverage this information to inform your own future content.

Don't forget: If it's online, it will be seen.

Don't follow the trend.

Don't copy and paste. What Just because it works for one company, it doesn't mean it will work for you, as shown in a few examples in this book. However, we encourage taking inspiration from industries other than your own. Umpqua Bank did this well: they looked outside banking to Starbucks to craft their unique customer experience. Exploring how other companies are engaging with customers could provide inspiration and exciting unique offerings that your competitors have not thought about yet.

Don't forget: Standing out is better than fitting in.

Alignment is crucial.

Design the emotional customer experience your company wants to project. Then for the digital strategy, select the right channels and then create the context. Carefully craft posts in a complete manner first before anything is uploaded. The entire channel should be designed as an emotional experience for the audience, as shown in the five-prong 'Burberry Love' case study. If a new campaign is being launched, design the whole experience from the beginning, questioning what the overall goals are. (And, importantly: these should expand far beyond profits.)

Don't forget: View engagements as holistic experiences.

Your customers are your greatest asset.

Without them you have no reason to exist, so bring the audience along on the journey. Look at the *how* and, more importantly, understand *why* customers are responding to messages. Use the information the audience posts and the questions they ask to better understand what it is they are responding to and why. This is a great way to gain insights into what they value. Use the posts strategically to prototype early ideas with customers.

Don't forget: The customer!

We might not remember the details, but we will remember how it made us feel.

Like most disagreements or fights, we may not remember what was specifically said, but we will remember how it made us feel. Everything you do say and post should reinforce the core affect you want to create, the reason your company does what it does and the values that you represent. Through this clear, concise and compounded affect customers will truly remember your brand.

Never forget: Affect.

* * *

Keep these principles in mind as you move on to the following case study and to chapter 6, where we discuss digital strategy in the real world.

Affect in the aviation industry

This case study is about Brisbane Airport, a major international airport serving over 20 million passengers annually. It decided to engage at an emotional level to better understand foreign passenger groups. This case study focuses on emotionally benchmarking and understanding a foreign customer group in order to gather insights from their passenger experience. The results were then analysed, translated and implemented within the organisation to produce the world's first departure card app, catering to international travellers' needs.

THE CHANGING DYNAMICS OF TOURISM

There has been a resurgence in the tourism industry of Australia, giving rise to innovation efforts in this field. One such effort is specifically focusing on digital channels to enrich the travellers' experiences, due to the changing expectations of travellers. To date the focus has been on smart technology advancements through personalisation, context awareness and real-time monitoring.

Over a decade ago (in 2006), Tourism Australia launched the campaign 'So where the bloody hell are you?' after spending over AU$180 million on its creation. It featured various Australian characters preparing for international visitors to their towns, from pouring them a beer in an outback pub to model Lara Bingle emerging from the clear-blue water of Fingal Island in a bikini, asking the rest of the world, 'So where the bloody hell are you?' The controversial campaign was banned by the United Kingdom's Broadcasting Agency in 2007 due to the use of the word 'bloody'. It was declared a failure and pulled by Tourism Australia a mere two years later.

There was backlash from around the world, as the message just got lost in translation. After all, what Japanese tourists want is completely different from the desires of an American tourist, right? The digital hedonic rhetoric of the campaign was to create a 'uniquely Australian invitation'. However, such a personalised invitation was broadcast via TV, billboards, magazines and mass cinema press showings—anything but personalised! A more strategic use of digital channel selection and design could have made the world of difference—especially to Mr Morrison, the member of Australian Parliament who lost his job at Tourism Australia over it!

The fact remains that this campaign went through a lot of market testing and focus groups all over the world before it was released. Such focus groups were held globally by various marketing consultants and it showed that people from around the world were not offended by the use of the word 'bloody'. So what went wrong? Figure M shows the break in the framework where the digital hedonic rhetoric and the digital stimulus do not align. This market is worth AU$17 billion to our nation, so you would think it's worth getting right from the beginning.

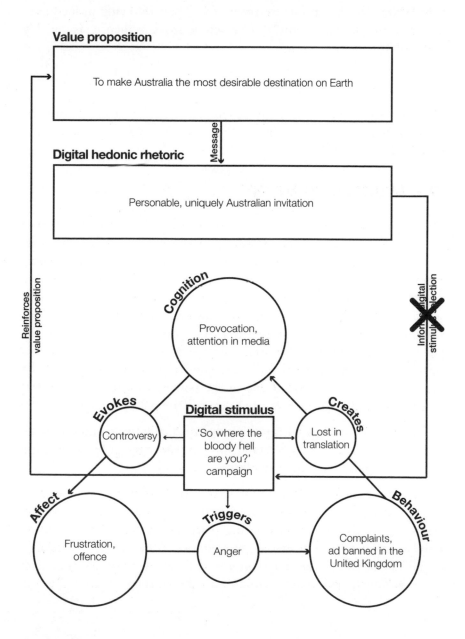

Figure M: framework breakdown: Tourism Australia's wrong channel selection

Obviously hindsight is a wonderful thing when it comes to innovation. However, some of the best ideas do get lost in the stimulus part of translation. This is a prime example of a great idea being pushed onto mainstream platforms purely to reach a mass audience as quickly as possible.

* * *

This case study shows an organisation that was not satisfied with the existing digital channels on the market—so they designed and created their own.

THE AVIATION INDUSTRY

The airport industry sits within aviation as a vital infrastructure service that makes air transportation possible. A traditional view is that airports are designed and exist to service airlines, considered to be the airport's major client due to the prioritisation of aeronautical revenue to airline operation. Typically, the passenger is viewed as the end user or customer to whom the value of an airport's operation is delivered. So through the traditional lens of an airport-to-airline customer segmentation, the passenger is viewed by an airport as a customer's customer. However, this notion is changing, as passengers are increasingly being considered the prioritised customer segment due to the potential for non-aeronautical revenue coupled with the pressure of immediate public perception.

Based on this change within the industry, qualitative market research approaches that deeply understand foreign passenger groups are being explored by most Australian airports.

An airport can be a confusing and stressful environment for passengers, where negative emotions are exacerbated under constant time pressure. Airports can also be a very exciting place, associated with adventure, holidays away, or new business opportunities. A passenger's experience within an airport is most commonly defined by activities that take place within the passenger terminal. So the passenger terminal is the primary touchpoint for interaction between passengers and the airport. Passenger experience is measured by service quality surveys, and it is the responsibility of airports and government bodies to regularly undertake these surveys. However, perceived quality can vary according to cultural and personal values, adding complexity to the surveys. The challenge for airports is to provide the best possible experience to all passengers in order to leave a lasting positive impression of a city and region and ensure that many more passengers return, using an airport by choice.

Airports frequently measure customer satisfaction in relation to functional aspects, such as passenger processes, airport facilities and customer services (as seen in figure N). However, the emotional aspects of the customer experience are rarely measured, if at all. While many companies have satisfaction goals and strategies, only a few rigorously measure their customers' satisfaction, and even fewer act upon the results.

Figure N: the Changi Airport toilets

But what exactly do passengers value? And how can this value be translated into superior airport performances? New technologies have revolutionised the way companies interact and engage with customers, and are providing new challenges and opportunities to solve existing problems. Airports, like most companies, have been unsure how to best seize the opportunities that digital channels present. For most companies, the difficulty has not been in developing and launching their digital initiatives, but making them truly engaging and valuable to their customer base.

The shift into non-aeronautical revenue requires more attention to be focused on customer satisfaction, with research revealing emotional experiences correlate to passengers being calm and comfortable, which in turn leads to repeat business, higher spending rates and ultimately increased revenue. Numerous airports globally have commenced developing digital channels such as mobile apps, social media platforms and interactive wayfinding maps as a way to create a better experience for the passenger. However, little is known about how airports use digital channels and their impact on passenger experience, with most studies focusing on wait times, safety and management of airport services as indicators of passenger satisfaction and experience. However, only through understanding travellers' needs and experiences can vendors learn how to best utilise technology.

DIGITAL TRENDS AT AIRPORTS

Within the airport sector the development of digital channels to enrich the passenger experience is slowly becoming sought after, due to passenger expectations and airport business goals both changing. This has placed an airport's digital channel strategy at the forefront, becoming a major consideration in the future management of airports. The continual pursuit of non-aviation focused innovation has seen the passenger and their experience become a major area of importance. The growth in digital channel adoption has allowed airports to gain competitive advantage through innovative offerings to passengers.

However, there is a limited understanding of how airports are currently applying digital channels strategically, and the influence this has on their overall service ratings. According to the SITA Airport IT Trends Survey, in 2013 airports invested US$6 billion on information technology, prioritising investment in passenger processing technology, and in improvements to passenger services and information. The survey revealed that business travellers requested day-of-travel notifications pushed to their phones, and more than 70 per cent wanted to receive alerts when their flight was boarding. The survey also found that a majority of business travellers were dissatisfied with airport wi-fi (which makes it tough for any digital channel to be used), and would prefer mobile boarding capabilities.

Recently, international airports have deployed airport mobile apps, which provide passengers with information related to their flight, as well as notifications of changes in travel details. Dallas/Fort Worth International Airport has also implemented large digital touchscreens within airport terminals, allowing passengers to find restaurants and amenities within a five-minute walk. Dallas/Fort Worth aims to have these 'digital wayfinders' across the entire airport by 2018.

Self-service processing is also trending in airport technology. Numerous airports have adopted self-check-in kiosks and self-service scanners, allowing passengers to check into and board flights without the need for staff. Recently, the International Air Transport Association (IATA) developed the 'Fast Travel' initiative in response to customer demands for greater self-service options. Customers will soon have the ability to print boarding passes at home, print and attach a bag tag at a dedicated airport kiosk, drop off their bags at an unattended bag drop station, and board aircraft through an automated self-boarding gate. This technology has already been introduced at several European airports, and is quickly trending in the airport technology arena.

THE STUDY

To understand how industrialised and capital-intensive industries use digital channels, we explored the 100 top-ranked airports in the world to explore how and for what purpose they are using digital channels. The aim was simple — to investigate the integration of company strategy with appropriate digital channels. The findings suggest that the purpose and content of current airport digital technologies do influence the service quality provided to passengers. Some airports are currently not using digital channels to their full extent; we will explain more on this as the case study unfolds. The study outcomes provided Brisbane Airport, in particular, with information on current digital channel use and penetration, thus enabling it to benchmark its performance across digital channels. The subjects of the analysis were a mix of airports rated highest, mid and lowest for passenger satisfaction.

The airports studied were chosen based on the 2015 Skytrax Airport Awards for Service Quality, which look at how travellers from over 160 countries perceive airport service quality. This large and prestigious customer satisfaction survey looks at the passenger experience throughout the 550 airports worldwide, detailing check-in and security through to departure. The survey runs from June to February the following year, and is based on the opinions of over 13 million passengers. From this survey the top 100 airports were selected and ranked in order. This allowed us to examine the contrasts between higher-rated airports and their choices of digital channels. This section shows the content analysis and classifies the digital touchpoints adopted.

All digital channels across the 100 airports were analysed. The average number of digital channels used was 9.1, with fifth-ranked Hong Kong International Airport using the most (18) and number 34, Shanghai Hongqiao, using the least: one. The most frequently used digital touchpoints across all airports (shown in figure O) were websites (100 per cent), Facebook (85 per cent), digital media releases (82 per cent) and Twitter (79 per cent). Additionally, 66 per cent had web enquiry, 64 per cent had LinkedIn, 53 per cent had access to a direct email address and just under half (49 per cent) had a mobile app. Touchpoints that were not used by any airports included tutorials, Reddit, Vimeo, digital catalogues and digital loyalty programs.

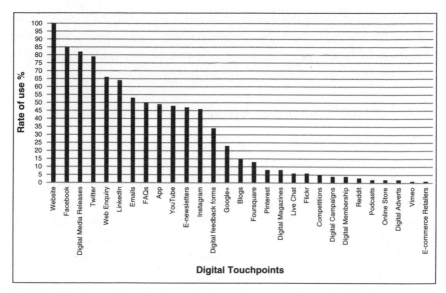

Figure O: rate of usage of digital touchpoints across 100 airports

No correlation was found between the age and size of airports in regard to their channel usage, however different locations saw differences in the use of digital channels. Airports in Asia had the lowest use rate of Facebook, LinkedIn, Twitter and Instagram. All three airports in South Africa used exactly the same digital channels: websites, mobile applications, web enquiry, LinkedIn, Facebook, Twitter, Foursquare and blogs.

The digital touchpoints of each airport were analysed in regard to the four digital channel typologies (functional, social, community and corporate). The top 10 airports overall had similar rates of usage across the typologies, including an average of 54 per cent for functional, 40 per cent for social, 28 per cent for community and 28 per cent for corporate. This largely remained consistent for the remaining airports; the largest drop was for both community and corporate typologies amongst the airports ranked eleventh to thirtieth, with a rate of 13 per cent for both.

In comparing the highest-ranked airport and the lowest, there was a drop from the use of 13 touchpoints across the four typologies to the use of seven touchpoints across three typologies. Another finding was the relation of typologies to the location of the airports: the Middle East had the highest rate of functional and social typologies, South Africa had the highest use of the community typology, while Europe was the highest for the use of the corporate typology. South America had the lowest use of functional, Asia was the lowest in social, Oceania overall lowest for community.

THE AIRPORT'S CHALLENGE

The rise of Asia presents a significant opportunity for the global business community. However, tailoring businesses to deliver value to different consumer groups is a challenge, given the size of the population and cultural diversity across Asia. Airports regularly collect and monitor quantitative data, so they have the ability to understand these customer segments through the passenger movement records captured in day-to-day operations. Quantitative data broken down into nationality segments can inform strategic decisions made by airport management as to how the airport will grow while optimising existing operational capacity.

Airports that seek to understand Chinese consumers through the segmentation of Chinese markets have traditionally approached the task through the geographic location of residence and income levels. This is considered a generic approach that segments Chinese consumers based on urban or regional residence and north or south geographic location within the country. Such a broad approach makes it challenging to understand and anticipate rapid cultural developments that affect consumer behaviour. Personal wealth and increasing global engagement are producing Chinese consumers who express their status through high-end luxury brands. Predicting the travel behaviour of the unknown Chinese consumer is considered difficult, given the customer segment's growing engagement in individualism. While the Chinese nationality segment is one target consumer group, there is a greater opportunity to develop research methods that can be applied to anticipate the future needs of other emerging customer segments.

Brisbane Airport was suffering a decline in retail revenue on the airside of the airport (past the security gates). It knew that a large segment of travellers from Asia were indeed purchasing many retail items from their visit to Australia, and wanted to know what new product mix to cater for in the retail airport environment. So it had commissioned a marketing consulting firm to conduct a large quantitative study on product preferences from the passengers in the hope that by stocking a new product mix it would stem the retail revenue decline.

AN EMOTIONAL DESIGN APPROACH

An emotional design approach aims to help businesses successfully innovate, differentiate and compete in a global marketplace. It is broadly defined as an approach that allows a company to consider and evaluate radically new propositions from multiple perspectives, typically spanning user needs, business requirements and technology demands (see figure 1.1, on page 4).

Emotional design methods (in this case study) are seen as an intimate shared understanding of the latent, current and future needs of the customer. As customers play an important role in the development of products and services, they must not just be seen as a source of information but also as a contributor with knowledge and skills. Active customers in the development process produce ideas that are significantly more innovative than those generated through traditional marketing techniques. A method to reveal such insights is not to question the how, what and where, but why certain consumer decisions are made.

The key is building a deeper emotional understanding of customer meaning and value, rather than being pulled by user requirements. Many of the methods used originate from a user-centred design approach and include user observations, scenarios of use, task analysis, personas and storyboarding. The aims of these methods are to uncover the needs and interests of the user, influencing the product's usability and understanding. These tools allow companies to connect and create value with their customer, extending beyond just pleasing a customer's superficial needs. Unlike marketing methods, the goal is not to evaluate a particular feature or experience of an existing product or service, but understand the customers' 'why'. The use of these methods allows a firm to place itself in the position of the customer, not by questioning their needs, but by trying to understand their values. Design techniques offer a more collaborative and creative engagement between the customer and a representative of an organisation, building a rapport that leads to deeper knowledge sharing. In this collaborative setting, converting a passive view of the customer into an active role can provide opportunities to imagine new market offerings with greater customer value.

Gathering customers' emotional insights can fulfil the role of qualitatively measuring performance or customer experience quickly, with an emphasis on building understanding through empathy. It is important to have a deep and personal empathy with customers as people, rather than as demographic or marketing categories. Such methods are low-risk alternatives to market research that focus on improving the lives of customers, not just exploring a typical business-to-customer transaction.

DESIGNING A BESPOKE DIGITAL CHANNEL

The Brisbane Airport project began with a problem statement: Decline in retail performance on airside of airport. We were engaged to understand international segments, spending breakdowns, store popularity and brand popularity based on point of sale data. Chinese customers were identified as the strategic focus for the airport based on passenger growth forecasts. Market research also revealed the brands and stores popular with Chinese nationals, including Louis Vuitton, Chanel and Prada, so the data suggested that the airport should introduce a set of luxury retail stores. Over a three-month period we applied a design approach to understanding the motives of the Chinese passengers as they passed through the airport.

The emotional insights we gathered held implications for the general operation of the airport and became the basis for idea generation. The original problem was then reframed to: 'eliminating the cultural barriers to security and customs checkpoints in the airport'. It turned out that the decline in retail performance was part of a much wider problem concerning the overall customer experience of Chinese nationals within the environment.

What would typically occur was that the Chinese national would purchase their products on the land side of the airport (prior to check-in and security), then begin to go through security and customs. They were often unaware as they queued up for security that they were carrying too much liquid. (The limit on international flights out of Brisbane is 500 millilitres.) This would cause conflict as security would inform them that they needed to throw out some of their recently purchased liquid items. This would occur with a large language barrier, holding up the queue. Security guards told us that this would occur daily. In addition, as the majority of these Chinese nationals did not speak English, many of them would struggle filling out their customs departure cards in English or get sent back by the customs officer for filling it out in Chinese. See figure P for the outgoing passenger card.

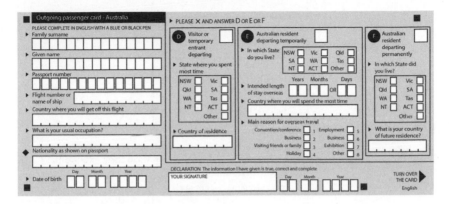

Figure P: mandatory outgoing passenger card

Note: Under Australian law, all international travellers heading out of Australia are required to fill in an 'outgoing passenger card', declaring in English where they're going, why and for how long.

Again, they would hold up the queue of other travellers and cause congestion. This experience left many Chinese nationals emotionally frazzled, frustrated and red-faced at the end of this experience—not to mention the time lost (time that could have been spent in the airside retail environment of the airport).

Three streams of insights were built upon to develop a culturally sensitive airport experience for Chinese passengers. The solution recognised that retail engagement was part of a total airport experience and that the act of driving retail performance could also support the general operational performance of the airport.

Figure Q (overleaf) visualises the process of moving from problem to solution and highlights how the project grew from a simple problem statement to an integrated solution.

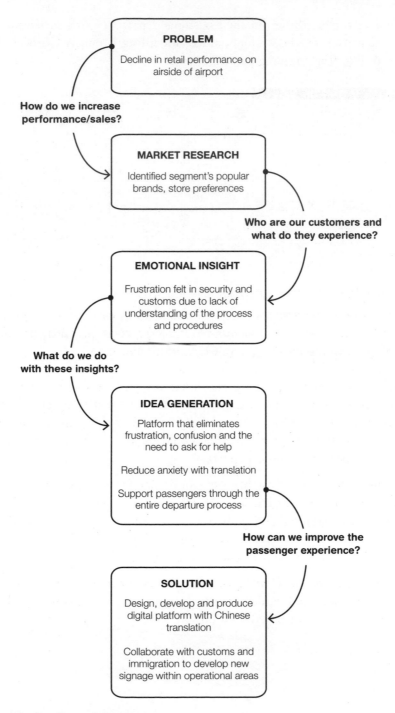

Figure Q: project stages

DESIGNING A DIGITAL SOLUTION

One solution to the newly uncovered problem was that of a digital departure card. This allowed for international passengers to complete the federally regulated card in their national language, then convert it into English and print it at a kiosk in the international terminal, all enabled by QR code technology.

The new digital departure card was built within the Brisbane Airport's existing mobile app, allowing passengers to use their mobile device to enter and save personal information to upload to the departure card prior to arrival at the airport. The card is then printed at the terminal, signed by the passenger, and taken by customs officers as part of the normal departure process. Passengers can also save their profiles, and those of their family members, within the app to use those details for their next international departure from Brisbane.

Digital solution breakdown

Step 1—Download the Brisbane Airport app.

Step 2—Select the departure tab.

Step 3—Enter your information.

Step 4—Bring your mobile phone with you to the airport.

Step 5—Go to the international terminal and visit the departure card kiosk near the security inspection area. Open your phone and locate the QR code saved in the 'My Trip' section of your Brisbane Airport app, scan the code at the kiosk and print a pre-populated departure card.

Step 6—Sign the card and enter the security and customs gates.

See figure R (overleaf) for a visual breakdown of the process.

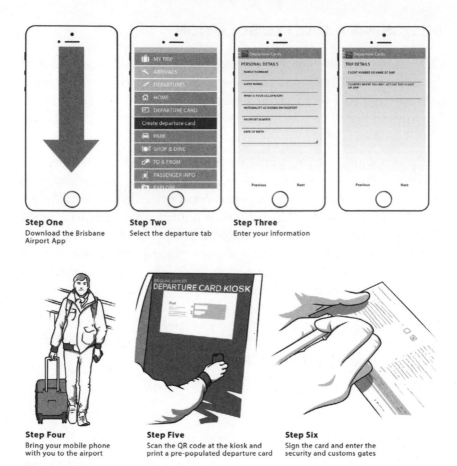

Step One
Download the Brisbane
Airport App

Step Two
Select the departure tab

Step Three
Enter your information

Step Four
Bring your mobile phone
with you to the airport

Step Five
Scan the QR code at the kiosk and
print a pre-populated departure card

Step Six
Sign the card and enter the
security and customs gates

Figure R: digital solution breakdown

The Brisbane Airport digital strategy led to the creation of this unique digital channel through the Digital Affect Framework seen in figure S.

'The result', says Julieanne Alroe, Brisbane Airport Corporation CEO, 'is an Australian (if not a world) first digital solution that will save time, streamline processing and help reduce anxiety associated with departure formalities, especially for non–English speaking travellers.'

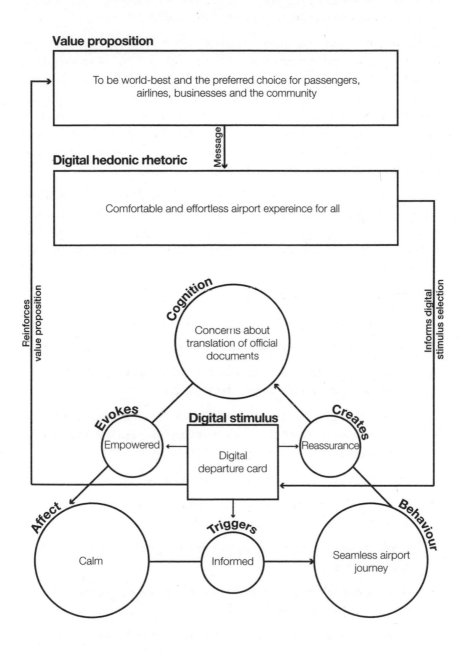

Figure S: Brisbane Airport Digital Affect Framework

This strategy was adopted by all areas of the organisation, where previously there was ambiguity in the form of many discrete and isolated digital channels belonging to separate departments.

The organisation has since received industry recognition for its initiative as a digital strategy leader. The mobile app was awarded 'Best in Class' at the Global Interactive Media Awards 2015, and it got one of the highest scores for any airport app ever (26/30) on the Moodie Reports APPraisal 2015. The airport received the 'Best Airport in Australia/Pacific' award at the Skytrax World Airports Awards, and it earned the 2015 Brisbane City Council Digital Strategy Innovation Award for its digital strategy leadership.

Their digital business strategy now underpins daily value creation. Since the project's completion the airport has launched multiple products and services that align to its digital business strategy. This is a classic Fox approach, with the bravery and foresight to strike out and design its own digital channel — making them market leaders.

Key lessons from Brisbane Airport

- Don't jump directly into pre-existing digital channels.

- Design the experience you want to create for the audience first.

- Don't use a cookie-cutter approach — what has worked for another organisation may not work for you.

- Select the digital channel that will elicit the emotion you want to achieve — and if there is not one out there, design one that does what you want.

- Understand the *why* beyond the face value.

- Benchmark other digital strategies and channels in the same industries.

- Look to other industries to inspire your digital channel selection and experience.

- It is not only about the channel but about how people use it — and if they will use it at all!

- Assess the value the channel brings the user and also the organisation.

CHAPTER 6

Managing affect: Digital strategy in the real world

Hopefully by this point we have demonstrated that pursuing customer insights and investing in both the process of designing digital channels and the digital channels themselves has a great impact on the customer–company relationship. Scaling this relationship depends on the customers' willingness to provide and share positive company experiences with others, which in turn enables the creation of engaging interactions via digital channels with customers, impacting company growth via revenue and the customers' emotional investment (advocacy) in the company.

This process requires a combination of creativity, deep emotional understanding, knowledge of digital behaviour and a strong company-to-customer strategy. Thus, the need for a formalised framework—the Digital Affect Framework—that includes customer motivations and requirements in designing for the desired behavioural results.

The framework alone, however, is not enough—you need to be able to translate this into the real world. Here are the two main ingredients for managing affect (the hardest bit):

1. the people (Who should lead this digital relationship and drive change?)

2. the principles to implementation (Where do I start and how do I manage this customer-centric perspective?).

INNOVATING THE BIGGER PICTURE

Langdon Morris argues that while

> one set of products and services may be exceptionally well-suited to the market at a particular point in time, it's rare for a company to successfully adapt its products and services to changing market conditions quickly enough to sustain the leadership position.

Companies that focus only on products are most likely to fail, as successful innovation requires many types of innovation. In order to explore this concept further we add emotional design to the analysis of two of the largest information technology companies in the world: Apple and Samsung. We will now compare the approaches of these two companies in detail through the lens of Larry Keeley's 10 types of innovation, exposing interesting emotional insights into their innovation processes.

Keeley's research aims to develop a systematic approach to the innovation process. He and his co-authors analysed the patterns of successful innovation in a specific industry and then made conscious, considered choices to innovate in a particular way. Their 10 types of innovation are structured into three categories:

1. configuration (profit model, network, structure and process)

2. offering (product performance and product system)

3. experience (services, channel, brand and customer engagement).

Their innovation spectrum moves from an internal focus to a customer focus, and aims to encourage companies to mix and match innovation, as 'using more types of innovation produces more sophisticated and surprising results—and does so in a way competitors can't easily spot or copy'.

Understanding customer motivations and company value is key to all business innovation types. This understanding requires a formalised process model (such as the Digital Affect Framework) that outlines all design components and drivers of innovation, and guides all company decisions across configuration, offering and experience. However, it all starts with first understanding why the company exists, and why it is important to the customer.

Research similarly illustrates that there are many different avenues to innovation, arguing that a single avenue should not be approached in isolation but as a holistic system. Morris identifies 38 distinct opportunities for innovation within an organisation, and it is argued that an organisation's individual components are not as important as the way they work together to enable the organisation to create and deliver value to its customers.

We believe, however, that a company should go beyond simply mixing and matching innovation types and step deeper into the emotional understanding of each aspect of the Keeley model (configuration, offering, experience) or of each innovation type. The emotional understandings of these three categories should then align and be incorporated into a holistic business strategy.

An integrated approach to emotional innovation can be found in the co-creation of products, services and experiences jointly by companies with their stakeholders, opening a whole new world of value. This is illustrated through the following example, comparing Samsung's and Apple's innovation and digital customer engagement in the smartphone arena.

The mobile communications industry, which includes many large companies with experienced customer bases, is highly aggressive and competitive. The fast-paced development of technology and the regular introduction of new products have significantly increased the capabilities of the electronic devices that characterise this industry. The main competitive factors in this industry include:

- price
- product features
- relative price/performance
- product quality and reliability
- design innovation
- third-party software
- marketing and distribution
- company reputation
- service
- support.

The profit model of technology companies is characterised by aggressive pricing practices, frequent product introduction, evolving technologies, and rapid adoption of technology and product advancements. For three years, Apple and Samsung have been involved in a history-making legal battle spanning four continents and costing in excess of a billion dollars.

Apple

Apple was established in California in 1977. Today, it designs and manufactures hardware (iPhone, Apple Watch, iPad, Mac and iPod) and software (iOS, iCloud, OSX and iTunes); provides online services; and distributes digital content and applications through its various outlets (iTunes Store, App Store, iBooks Store and Apple Pay). Apple's business strategy is 'committed to bringing the best user experience to its customers through its innovative hardware, software and services'. This strategy leverages its ability to design and develop its own operating systems, hardware and application software and services. It ensures 'a high-quality buying experience with knowledgeable salespersons who can convey the value of the complement of Apple's offerings', believing that this strategy greatly enhances its ability to attract and retain customers.

Apple primarily manages its business on a geographic basis, appealing to its customers in the Americas, Europe, Greater China, Japan and the Asia-Pacific. The company makes most of its revenue through the sale of electronic devices that consumers perceive as superior to those made by its competitors, and by creating strong emotional user experiences. In addition, a seamless digital experience is not limited to Apple devices but is consistently found across all touchpoints of its products, services and stores.

Apple's business is configured to offer innovation in and integration of its entire technology solution, including hardware, software and online services. The sale of its products and technologies relies on continued minimal investment in research and development. Apple's success depends largely on its continued capability to create innovative products and services for each of the markets in which it competes. It also standardises pricing across its product range, and controls all discount offerings.

Apple's products and services employ the same operating system, providing a consistent experience across its product and service range, ease of use and integration. In June 2007, Apple entered the smartphone market for the first time; just three years later, it was the most profitable handset vendor, posting a net profit of US$1.6 billion, exceeding (then) world-market leader Nokia's profit by US$0.5 billion.

The iPhone is perceived as superior to its competitors, being described as a combination of functional, usable and brilliant design. Nokia tried to compete at a product level with its N95, which was released the same year as the original iPhone and surpassed the latter's 2-megapixel camera with a 5-megapixel camera with flash. The 2010 iPhone 4 finally caught up to competitors' 5-megapixel cameras; by this time, however, many competitors (such as Nokia, Sony, Ericsson and Samsung) had already launched smartphones with 8-megapixel cameras. However, these rivals were competing on product, and this was not enough to gain market supremacy: users were still demanding iPhones.

Apple's business model was created to use both hardware (smartphones) and software (the App Store) to deliver its services, making its offerings accessible to a mass market. However, Apple has faced substantial competitive pressure from other companies that are promoting and providing their own digital content, including video and peer-to-peer music streaming.

As for Apple's customer engagement, the devil is in the detail. From the calculated design of the air pocket inside the perfect white packaging of its devices to the warranty card and SIM ejector pin, there is no denying the unique way in which Apple designs a delightful customer encounter. Thus, Apple has an extremely strong brand identity and strategy that is focused on emotion.

More specifically, Apple's brand personality is about lifestyle, imagination, and empowering consumers through technology that is simple to use and complexity-free. It is a much-loved brand and has a community of 'Apple Addict' followers. In New York City, on 19 May 2001, for example, a queue began forming twelve hours before Apple's flagship store opened on Fifth Avenue. It was comprised of more than a thousand avid Apple cultists, some even camping out overnight. In a poll by brandchannel.com, participants voted Apple as the brand with the greatest impact on their lives, the most inspiring brand, and the one they 'cannot live without'. Customers don't simply buy Apple products; they buy into the brand.

Apple sells its products worldwide through retail stores, online stores and direct sales, as well as through third-party cellular network carriers, wholesalers, retailers and value-added resellers. In addition, through its online and retail stores, the company sells a variety of third-party iPhone-, iPad-, Mac- and iPod-compatible products, including application software and various accessories. It sells to mainstream consumers, small and midsized businesses and education facilities, and various enterprises and governments.

Through Apple's retail stores, prospective customers are given an unwavering display of the company's brand values as they enter a stimulating environment and discover more about the Apple family, 'test drive' and receive training, and receive practical help with Apple products at the shops' 'Genius Bars'. Apple's retail staff are enthusiastic, informative and helpful, showing their dedication to the brand without being sales-driven or pushy (as they are not paid by commission). As advocates for the brand themselves, they take pride in the pre- to post-sales and support services they provide. Indeed, the 'Mac Community' kept the company alive during the 1990s, a turbulent period in Apple's history. Since then, members of this community have been users of Apple's main product lines, and enable the company to sustain pricing that is at a premium compared to its competitors' (see figure 6.1).

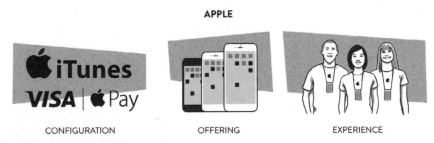

APPLE

CONFIGURATION OFFERING EXPERIENCE

Figure 6.1: Apple's approach to innovation

Samsung

Samsung was founded in 1938, in Seoul, South Korea. By 2009, the company was the world's largest IT company, with the business separated into three areas:

1. consumer electronics (visual displays, digital appliances, printing solutions, health and medical equipment)

2. IT and mobile communications (smartphones, tablets and watches)

3. device solutions (memory systems and business solutions).

Today, it is known globally for its electronic products, and has become one of the most successful brands in the electronics and information technology industry, building products in-house to meet predetermined price and feature requirements.

In the 1980s, the few designers who worked for the company were scattered through the engineering and new product development departments. In Samsung, efficiency, competence and engineering rigour were valued highly, and these designers had little influence or say apart from input into the aesthetic of the product. In 1996, however, the chairman of the Samsung Group, Lee Kun-hee, instigated a 'design revolution' in the company. The first response was to outsource the best Korean designer to take over the design function of all products. However, executives convinced Lee to instead focus on nurturing the company's internal designers to develop an organisation-wide design capability.

Today, Samsung employs 1600 designers and the innovation process is based on research conducted by 'multidisciplinary teams of designers, engineers, marketers, ethnographers, musicians and writers who search for users' unmet needs and identify cultural, economic and technological trends'. As innovative as this approach is, challenges still exist: its efficiency-focused management practices, driven by tech-engineering mindsets in the organisation, create difficulties in shifting to an innovation-centric culture.

Samsung's value proposition is 'to devote our talent and technology to creating superior products and services that contribute to a better global society'. Supporting this value proposition are the company's five value principles: people, excellence, change, integrity and co-prosperity. The business vision strategy for 2020 is to 'inspire the world, create the future; reaching $400 billion in revenue and to become one of the world's top five brands'.

Samsung's vertical business structure is split into three different business divisions; this structure has formed a competitive culture between departments, as the company seeks out the very best employees for all levels of management. Samsung's current strategy is hardware innovation and quick and frequent product launches. This strategy has not only created a competitive culture between employees of different divisions, but also floods the market with a myriad Samsung products in a short period of time. It also creates a wider customer base by offering a plethora of gadgets to both low- and high-end markets. Samsung products can easily be price discounted as it relies on third-party vendors to off-sell its stock.

Samsung's focus is on innovation and the development of 'next-generation' products (such as the curved TV). Its swift technology development constantly delivers a broad range of products to the market. The focus on hardware rather than software also means that all efforts and costs are invested in technology.

As a result of its wide range of products, Samsung does not match Apple in attention to minor industrial design details. For example, the microphone and speakers of the Galaxy smartphone are misaligned, while Apple's iPhone is perfectly aligned and crafted.

The wide diversity of Samsung products also creates challenges for its after-purchase and warranty servicing. For example, if a product fails, consumers need to take it back to the retailer who will replace it (if under warranty), or provide a service contact number or warehouse drop-off. However, such indirect contact with the product company has an impact on the overall customer support experience.

While Samsung relies on third-party retailers to sell its products, it also has a digital store and wholesalers through which it connects directly with customers. The company has recently focused on digital social channels such as Facebook, Twitter and Instagram to engage customers. Over the past four years, it has invested heavily in this area, and has successfully attracted over 42 million 'likes' on its Samsung Galaxy Facebook page. This garnering of support through social channels relates to Samsung's branding that is focused on the 'freedom to explore' and the drive to 'try new things'.

This branding also aligns to the company's focus on next-generation products, and the provision of choice to customers. Awareness of the brand has spread with the sponsorship of such events as the 2014 Winter Olympics and the Academy Awards. Samsung's customer engagement is not based on the provision of overwhelming general support, but on providing information on its products' features and technological superiority to guide customer decision making. Samsung's reputation and longevity also engages customers by indicating that it is a brand to be trusted, and that it is a company with the latest, greatest and on-going technological developments (see figure 6.2).

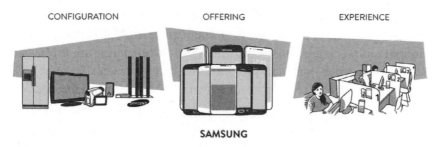

Figure 6.2: Samsung's approach to innovation

Configuration

Apple and Samsung have completely different configurations. Apple is able to keep research and development and cost of revenue expenses relatively low, as most aspects of the hardware (component production and assembly) are outsourced. Margins are kept high by focusing on a limited and sleekly designed premium-priced product to showcase its featured software architecture. These products are then skilfully advertised and promoted to not only sell the individual product, but also to inform customers of the whole Apple system (for example, other products and services such as iTunes and Apple Pay).

Samsung's strategy, on the other hand, is a high level of vertical integration through the high-revenue area of semiconductor and component businesses feeding to multiple downstream product markets. Samsung has overpowered its competitors over the past 20 years by outspending them in most areas of the value chain, particularly in research and development, capital expenditures, marketing and promotion, and sales channels.

Offering

Apple has control over all its offerings, from the design of its hardware and software to the retailing of these products. Even network operators are chosen and contracted by Apple to exclusively promote the iPhone. Apple also controls the content of its iTunes store, thus securing a strong position as a regulator of the entire product system.

Samsung released 116 different models of smartphone from June 2009 to August 2015, compared to Apple's release of 10 iPhones from 2007 to September 2014. Samsung's frequent level of new releases across its three business divisions could be the reason for its higher sale rates compared to Apple.

Historically, seasonal holiday demand increases Apple's net sales in the first quarter, with new product releases also significantly influencing net sales, product costs and operating expenses. This is due to the anticipation that consumers and distributors create around new product releases.

In September 2015, Apple released Apple TV, which claimed to bring 'a revolutionary experience to the living room based on apps built for the television'. Eddy Cue (Apple's senior vice-president of internet software and services) stated that 'there has been so much innovation in entertainment and programming through iOS apps, we wanted to bring the same excitement to the television'.

Since Steve Jobs' death in 2011, Apple has slowly and systematically made decisions surrounding innovation that Jobs himself proclaimed he would never consider. Such examples include the release of an iPad with a smaller screen in 2012 and a stylus called the 'Apple Pencil' in 2015. In 2010, Jobs commented on the size of Samsung's Galaxy S series smartphone, saying that 'you can't get your hand around it', and 'no one's going to buy that'. However, in 2014, Tim Cook (the current CEO of Apple) released the iPhone 6 Plus, with the same screen size as its Samsung Galaxy competitor.

Experience

In 2013 and 2014, Apple was ranked as the 'best global brand' while, in the same period, Samsung jumped from number eight to seven. The increase in brand rating for Samsung could be attributed to its new design focus, its connection with customers via social channels, and its investment in public events to increase exposure and build brand awareness. Perhaps knowing it is unable to directly compete with Apple, Samsung has chosen to invest in areas that Apple has either ignored or limited its investment in.

Apple's strategy focuses on changing the meaning of its products, while Samsung competes by providing the most up-to-date and innovative hardware developments. An example of this is Apple's iPod. It was not the first music player on the market; however, it was able to change the meaning and experience of listening to music. Not only was it a well-designed product, it connected customers to the wider product system that Apple offered and changed the way that customers access music via its novel iTunes interface.

Apple and Samsung both provide good design at a product level. However, Apple continues the notion of 'engagement' throughout its entire business model. Customers love the Apple brand because the experience is consistent: from the experience of walking into an Apple store, to the product, its packaging and its marketing. While Samsung can compete on a product level, it is unable to provide the same customer experience as Apple.

A JOB FOR A FOX

In the previous chapters, we looked at how Burberry considered emotions when designing their multichannel strategy, with support from the CEO and a sweeping digital campaign aimed at building a stronger customer relationship. Angela Ahrendts, the CEO at the time, reminded people that 'the universal language is not texted, emailed, or spoken. It is felt.' However, she also recognised that every company talked about building relationships with their customers, and in order for a firm the size of Burberry to actually execute on this promise they needed to start with the employees first. Few companies are so lucky! Too often it is left to one department to be the gatekeepers of the customer. If the management team are not supportive of more resources being used, if the expertise in emotional design itself are sub-contracted in, and if prototyping such radical customer propositions seems too risky, then all the design thinking sprints, post-it notes and sharpies in the world won't help you.

This book began with the introduction of two characters—the Hedgehog and the Fox.

Hedgehogs are leaders with vision; they think big. They take risks unwaveringly in order to get high-impact returns. Winston Churchill has been identified as a Hedgehog-like leader, with his strong personality and bold, unwavering vision that Britain would not just survive World War II, but prevail as a great nation.

Fast forward to our times and convert this to modern-day business acumen, and you cannot go past the example of Apple and the late, great Steve Jobs—also a Hedgehog. Many companies we have worked with over the past decade have spoken of the desire to be 'like Apple'. To have a brand like Apple, to have an in-store retail experience like Apple—however, the reality is that we cannot all be like Apple.

And what happens when the Hedgehog leader's vision is the wrong vision? In the case of Apple, even when the vision is bold and spot-on market-wise, the Hedgehog needs to acknowledge that their prickly style of management can prevent their bold vision from being executed successfully. Churchill knew his unapproachable, towering personality could possibly deter some facts from the front line from reaching him in their rawest form. So, at the beginning of the war he set up a separate department solely to report unfiltered information to him daily—outside the normal chain of command. Similarly, Apple in 1985 voted to fire Jobs, reporting that he was uncontrollable—'he gets ideas in his head, and then to hell with what anybody else wants to do'. However, in 1997, when Apple was operating at a loss and Microsoft's Windows 95 was flying off the shelves, the same board decided that uncontrollable visionary character was exactly what the company needed.

In comparison, Foxes play the odds—they may not win big and go for broke in their garage, but they would rarely cause a catastrophe.

Thousands of years ago Archilochus summed up this idea by saying 'The Fox knows many things, but the Hedgehog knows one big thing'. Now this parable has been the subject of much debate over the past 2500 years. Who will triumph over whom? Jim Collins took up the debate in his 2001 book *Good to Great*. According to Collins, organisations are more likely to succeed if they focus on one thing, and do that one thing very well. By doing so, they can beat their competitors and become, in his words, 'truly great businesses'. Great businesses emerge (according to Collins) through something called the Hedgehog concept, derived from three separate assessments:

1. What are you and your staff truly passionate about?

2. What do you do better than anyone else?

3. Where are you good at generating revenue?

The Hedgehog concept (see figure 6.3, overleaf) combines the three intersections representing the organisation's business strategy going forward.

We agree that this concept is definitely labelled correctly—it is exactly how hedgehogs operate, looking internally to derive strategy. This is exactly the description of a 'push' approach—'What do we have that we can sell customers?' Not 'What are our customer's problems and how can we make their lives better?' Their push approach to the marketplace and their self-indulgent behaviours will, the majority of the time, end in products and services no-one wants to buy.

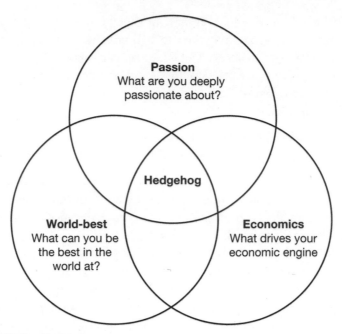

Figure 6.3: the Hedgehog concept

Source: Collins, 2001.

In contrast, the Fox concept (see figure 6.4) depicts an outward-looking approach. It begins with 'Who are my customers and what are they feeling? How can my company address these emotions?' Which leads to 'What digital technology platform do they want to be engaged on?' The digital age that we now live in has dramatically changed every aspect of our lives. The Hedgehog days are over and the Foxes are just beginning.

Figure 6.4: the Fox concept

A Fox should be appointed to translate and facilitate emotional insight, meaning and strategy into all facets of the organisation. In this role, they will need to continuously explore, instigate, challenge and disrupt customer relationships internally and externally. They extend on this process by re-aligning business activities and subsequently mapping these activities back to the strategy of the firm—continuously and iteratively prototyping solutions and shaping the central emotional value proposition of the firm. They should analyse and synthesise data, in order to draw out valid, nonspecific conclusions to help reframe problems. Early and continued stakeholder engagement and buy-in are essential, as by nature these findings seek to generate discussion, debate and perhaps controversy, in order to challenge 'the way it's always been done'. Foxes need to lead the way through design thinking traits such as emotional empathy with customers, digital design and ideation.

Table 6.1 shows both the Fox and the Hedgehog management styles.

Table 6.1: Hedgehog vs Fox management styles

Hedgehog management style	Fox management style
They have a strong sense of internally focused priorities	They derive priorities but are not afraid to change them
They have the ability to assess the energy levels required per task	They lead and inspire the energy levels by example per task
By nature, they are confident facilitators; they could 'sell ice to the Inuit'	By nature, they are complex and abstract thinkers
They can convince the room that design will solve the problem of the hour — no matter how wicked the problem	They think beyond enterprise boundaries through intellectual agility
	Sometimes this makes them aloof, however they take time to not jump to conclusions
They are flamboyant and experts with the solution. They don't hesitate to promise the solution, however when things go south they are quick to blame others	They are sometimes labelled 'opportunistic'
When design exercises are conducted they can direct and instruct, however when things come unstuck (for example when a group is not getting anywhere with the particular tool or approach) they are unable to spontaneously derive a unique way forward on the fly	They recognise that reality emerges from the interactions of many different agents and forces, including luck

Hedgehog management style	Fox management style
They can follow the process of design, convergent and divergent thinking — however the Hedgehogs witnessed have come up short on the final design result. When the complexity of some problems kicks in all they can do is to go back to the beginning and do the same things over again — yielding the same results	They often produce large and unpredictable outcomes that are of benefit but perhaps do not fit the original brief
They will frequently parrot others and not hesitate to make claims that are unsubstantiated	They have an open-minded approach to problem-solving
They have a theory about the world that resides within one framework in which every solution can be solved. There is no acknowledgement for other methods	The power of the Fox is in their willingness to try new things and their flexibility to accommodate others' ways of doing things
They bristle with impatience towards people who do not see things their way and are overconfident in their forecasts	They are cautious, more pragmatic and more inclusive to see complexity and nuances in the world around them
They are reluctant to admit error, opinionated and closed-minded	Foxes can assist a group in explaining how design tools work, demonstrate their use, as well as solving problems off the top of their head
Their strength is found in their focus on the central vision	The world is many, many shades of grey, and the Fox knows the subtle differences between them all
They drive and execute efficiency within an organisation via delegation	They have the ability to think like a hybrid in the physical and digital context simultaneously
They see the world in black and white	They think not only about the job to be done but the interrelating systems that surround that job

Having worked with many Foxes (and Hedgehogs) in industry, we have seen that their everyday value is an emotional, deeper understanding of customers, stakeholders and those managing them, by empathising with their customers and understanding the future and latent needs of the prospective customer. Furthermore, they provide companies with more emotionally aware innovation tools, processes and strategies, which enables them to better connect with their customers. The role of the Fox requires unbiased critical thinking, while aiming to understand and translate the human complexity of the business. This is especially vital as they connect and motivate separate departments of the organisation to work together to solve common and complex problems—a skill few possess.

IMPLEMENTING AFFECT

We are now going to reflect on the studies collected in this book through the lens of the three stages of implementation (configuring, offering and experience). These three stages serve as a set of 'ground rules' for practitioners and organisations looking to implement this theory.

Many projects are labelled as 'customer centric' when, frequently, design thinking approaches are being applied far too shallowly. This is the case, for instance, when design thinking is applied with no consideration of the organisational governance structures needed to influence and support such a business transformation. This in turn leads to such efforts resulting in few long-term benefits for an organisation and its stakeholders.

The underlying capability of design is that it employs a user-needs approach (empathy)—not only to the end-user (or consumer), but to partners' and stakeholders' needs also—providing a broader platform for radical innovation.

The inclusion of key stakeholders and partners as participants in the innovation process injects greater scope for participatory design. An 'outside-in' approach to business model innovation can be derived by integrating the values of relevant stakeholders and prototyping (and experimenting) with these possible future constructs. When design is added as an explorative lens in the innovation processes, businesses are better equipped to make sense of market opportunities and customer needs. However, design tends to be limited to the management arena and is often not leveraged at the higher strategic levels of a firm. It has to go beyond the digital styling of the channel and strategically support the customer relationship. Companies that don't fully understand the emotional drivers of their current and future customers risk missing new opportunities in the market and are vulnerable to disruption. Managing such activities can be chaotic at times, but the risks of not doing so are too catastrophic to ignore. This paired understanding of company digital strategy and customer emotion is the key to successful affective digital channels.

We propose that innovation requires insights into 'how' and 'why' customers behave, in order to deliver emotional digital engagements. Since emotions drive customer behaviour, starting with a clear emotional mission and value driver for customers is paramount. These three stages (as listed below) are framed to allow for step-by-step implementation.

Step 1: A Fox's company and customer strategy

Aligning and knowing your value involves understanding that the:

- underlying emotional driver of company strategy should be known and communicated

- company should be able to outline the purpose, values strategy and behaviour standards

- relationship between company identity and customer needs should be aligned

- emotions associated with the company strategy are supported by the right digital channel typology and touchpoints

- appropriate meaning being delivered is important in building equity in the company

- consistent communication of appropriate digital content that aligns with the company's strategy will design desired digital channel engagements.

All engagements with customers should reflect the meaning and value of the company's strategy and either match the customer need or align with their values.

To implement this step, the designer needs to work closely with all departments of the company to understand and disseminate the value and aligning emotions behind the company strategy. Employees need to know the emotional driver of the company and values to inform their communication strategies. By understanding what emotion you aim to evoke when a customer engages with a company, the right digital touchpoint can be designed.

This was particularly obvious in the example of Kodak, where the emotionally driven value proposition of 'share memories, share life' was overlooked as they focused on internal process innovation in order to reduce film processing time, missing the future digital Instagram wave where the photo was not the focus—the proposition of sharing memories was. A classic case of misalignment of emotionally driven strategy and innovation.

Step 2: A Fox understands needs

In step 2, the aim is to plan the design and purpose of digital channels to address customer needs and understand the way they are used by customers.

Designing digital channels involves:

- embracing new methods to understand your customers' needs

- the tools and skills to allow you to accurately interpret and articulate customer emotions into meaning and needs

- choosing the right digital touchpoint to communicate company value, while also addressing customer needs

- evoking feelings, emotions and moods that align with the brand and customer.

The successful use of customer needs requires a deeper analysis and engagement with customers through all stages of the project. Once customer needs are understood, the right channel can be designed to address these needs. A design approach should be applied for this, such as ideating, creating and testing the idea with customers. Findings from the first stage should be implemented into the process of designing the digital channel.

One case that we looked at was the Wii; Nintendo decided to change the market, revealing a completely different set of user needs to answer with their product. The graphics and games were inferior to those of its competitors, PlayStation and Xbox, but the games and interface were enjoyable for the whole family—it was a hit.

Step 3: The Fox's way to shaping behaviour

In step 3, the creation of positive experiences results in relaxed customers, which in turn results in repeat business, higher spending rates and ultimately increased revenues.

The digital channel experience involves understanding:

- designing for an emotional experience, not just a functional purchase behaviour

- the emotion targeted in the engagement has a positive long-term experience

- the action and behaviour you wish to create is beyond the transactional sale

- the overall experience is a positive and memorable one, leading to customer loyalty.

To implement this successfully, designers, marketers and strategists need to work together and place no ownership on customer engagements. Behaviour has a direct relation to the emotions evoked through the engagement, therefore this can only be achieved after the first two areas are successful. The digital channel engagement must also translate the company values and address customer needs.

This was demonstrated through the example of Meat Pack, the Guatemalan sneaker company. They were able to successfully 'steal' customers away from competitors located in the same shopping centre as they were, from one digital channel. The app on their smartphones gamified the shopping experience and made purchasing a pair of sneakers a race against time.

Final thoughts

Behind most business successes is a story about change—change in the market, change in the economy, or change in a particular product or service. To become a market leader, a company needs to act quickly on change, gain deeper insights into their entire operations, and learn about their customers. However, even though the pace of change continues to accelerate, emotional design innovation, a powerful tool to navigate change, is not well understood and is poorly practised. However, as firms build awareness of different innovation strategies, tools and processes, their ability to adopt and embed these within their organisations requires change at all levels of the business. This change demands not only strong leadership, but also a change in company culture and thinking. Long-term thinking and continual measurement of its impacts, both quantitative and qualitative, will help to ensure that organisational efforts will be sustained for the long term. It takes a systematic approach to achieve organisation-wide change. Nevertheless, leaders tend not to account adequately for systematic change, and they are surprised and unprepared when they should not be.

In the digital age, a greater emotional understanding of the world is required. Emotions govern behaviours, and designing for affect has been proven to strengthen customer relationships. We must learn to stop searching for the one correct, quantifiable answer. We must be less impressed by those Hedgehogs who say they have it, and more willing to support those Foxes who seek it. They are the ones who will lead us to an affected future.

A (very) brief history of emotions

The medical definition of emotion traditionally sees them as an instinctive response to external stimuli. Neuroscientist Antonio Damasio states that emotion has the biological function of regulating an organism's internal state so that it can be prepared for a specific reaction to suit a situation—particularly a dangerous situation. For example, the 'flight reaction' provides increased blood flow to the legs, facilitating running and escaping.

Many authorities have investigated different approaches to cognitive interpretation of human behaviour and the role emotions play in such tasks. Their studies firmly posit emotion as central to the cognitive reasoning process. Using magnetic resonance imaging (MRI), it was determined that emotions and cognition are unified and contribute to the control of thought and behaviour conjointly and equally.

Donald Norman is a strong advocate of emotion being a key component of cognition and the experience of the psychological objects around us. He asks why washing and polishing your car seems to make it drive better, and explores why attractive objects provide the sometimes illusory, sometimes real, effect of superior function. Review of the body of research on the topic reveals a general consensus that an individual reacts to the world through his or her emotions, and that stimuli such as arousal, action tendency and subjective feeling (pleasant or unpleasant) evoke emotions in all individuals.

If one accepts emotion as central to the cognitive-reasoning process, the question arises: how does emotional cognition differ from rational cognition or rational thought? As Damasio discusses, reason and logic—or intelligent thinking—are not separate from emotion but are an indelible part of every thought that is processed.

Damasio describes emotion as the antithesis to reason, and it was his studies that demonstrated the importance of emotion in decision making. A reason for this may be due to the emotional part of the brain being larger and tending to dominate over the rational brain to control the thought process. Evoking emotions can change the way we feel, and have a strong influence on our general experience of wellbeing. Emotions even affect which memories are stored and which are recalled: the stronger the emotion, the greater likelihood that the event will be placed into memory.

Donald Norman established that as part of the consumer's emotional response to a product, their affect results from an appraisal of a product and is based on the cognitive response (visceral, behavioural and reflective components of emotional cognition). Although affect and cognition are to some degree neuroanatomically distinct systems, they are also deeply intertwined. Processing at each level serves two different functions: evaluation or judgement of the world and things happening in it (affect); and the interpretation of what is happening in the world (cognition). Authorities agree that each system influences the other, with cognition leading to affect, and affect influencing cognition.

In Damasio's theory,[3] a typical case begins with thoughts and evaluations about the stimulus, and this mental activity triggers a bodily response (emotion). According to Damasio, these emotions are crucial in the decision making process and the choice of action (behaviour). The *as-if-loop* in the somatic feedback theory is the process of directly signally the brain (the amygdala and the prefrontal cortices) without the bodily activity actually occurring. Damasio explains 'this will generate a feeling more quickly and efficiently, although it may not feel the same as a genuine bodily response'.[4]

Digital Affect Framework canvas

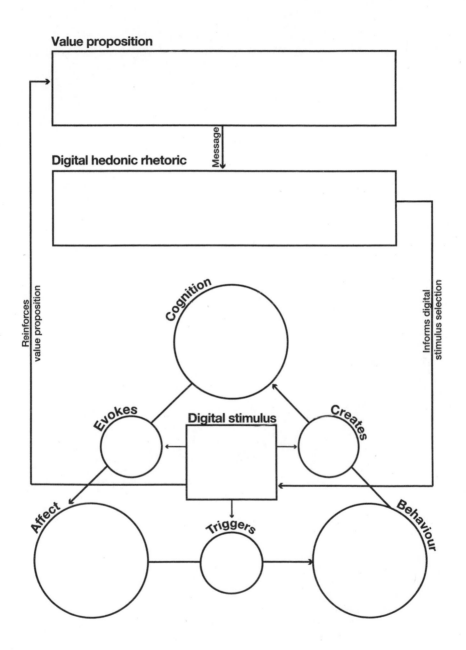

Typologies and touchpoints index

Typology	Criteria	Touchpoint	Content	Purpose	Direction	Interaction	Customer needs
Functional	Run by one user or company	Website	Information	Interaction Diversion Functional	Simplex	Medium	Quick, accessible company information with ability to respond to customer directed enquiries
	Medium to low customer interaction commonly through the ability to post comments, email enquiries or set up chat	Podcasts	Information	Interaction Functional	Simplex	Medium	No integration or connection or re-direction to other digital channels
		Tutorials	Support	Interaction Functional	Simplex	Medium	
		App	Information Revenue Promotion	Interaction Functional Diversion	Simplex	Medium	
		Online Store	Revenue	Functional	Simplex	Medium	
		Live Chat	Support	Interaction	Duplex	Medium	
		Web Enquiry	Support	Interaction	Duplex	Medium	
		E-News Letters	Information Promotion	Diversion	Simplex	Medium	
		Emails	Information Support	Interaction	Duplex	Medium	
		LinkedIn	Information	Interaction	Simplex	Medium	

		Platform	Information Promotion	Interaction Diversion			
Social	Run by an administrator with ability to delete and block users	Facebook	Information Promotion	Interaction Diversion	Duplex	High	Participation, sharing and collaboration to provide information
	High user interaction and ability to post and respond directly to comments in real time, limits on number of characters	Twitter	Information Promotion	Interaction Diversion	Duplex	High	High engagement between employees and customers and customers to customers
		Instagram	Information Promotion	Interaction Diversion	Duplex	High	Used only as advertisement and promotion channel, with lack of or no interaction between firm and customer comments
	They rely on user-created content and when these users interact or *like* a	Reddit	Information Promotion	Interaction Diversion	Duplex	High	
		Foursquare	Information Promotion	Interaction Diversion	Duplex	High	
	company or brand profile they often expect something in return.	Flickr	Information Promotion	Interaction Diversion	Duplex	High	Limited activeness across a number of touchpoints, leading to high level of customer-created content.
		Google+	Information Promotion	Interaction Diversion	Duplex	High	

(continued)

Typology	Criteria	Touchpoint	Content	Purpose	Direction	Interaction	Customer needs
Community	Run by an administrator, with features such as privacy settings	Forums	Information	Diversion	Duplex	Medium	Direct engagement with one employee and select community of customers, allowing for depth in information and communication across a community of customers with more specific interests
	Micro-blogging can post longer forms of text, with number of images and videos	Blogs	Information	Diversion	Duplex	Medium	
		YouTube	Information	Diversion	Duplex	Medium	
		Vimeo	Information	Diversion	Duplex	Medium	
	Customer can comment and rate the posts	Pinterest	Information	Diversion	Duplex	High	Content can be removed by touchpoint administrator if they infringe copyright or materials are not appropriate
							Also lack of engagement or activeness can lead to disconnection and loss of community.

		Touchpoint	Type			Level	Notes
Corporate	One way engagement from company to customer or customer to the company No cross interaction possible between company and customer	Digital media releases	Information	Functional	Simplex	Low	Gain customer feedback Support other channels
		Digital magazines	Information	Functional	Simplex	Low	Gain customer information, contact details.
		Digital catalogues	Information	Functional	Simplex	Low	Limited supporting touchpoints can lead customers to question transparency and trust of company
		Digital feedback forms	information	Functional	Simplex	Low	
		FAQ	Support	Functional	Simplex	Low	
		Digital advertisement	Information promotion	Functional	Simplex	Medium	
		Competitions	Promotion	Functional	Simplex	Medium	
		Digital campaigns	Promotion	Functional	Simplex	Medium	
		E-commerce retailers	Revenue	Functional	Simplex	Medium	
		Digital Membership	Information promotion	Functional	Simplex	Medium	
		Digital Loyalty Programs	Information promotion	Functional	Simplex	Medium	

Glossary of key terms

Affect: what we feel. 'Affect' is used to describe the topics of emotions, feelings and moods collectively, triggering a bodily response.

Affect eliciting conditions: a list of affective states described through the conditions they produce, synthesised from Desmet.[5]

Affective state classification: a process of analysing a company's value proposition into a digital hedonic rhetoric code.

Behaviour: what we do. Behaviour is the choice of action triggered by affect.

Behavioural reactions: the actions one engages in when experiencing a change in core affect.

Cognition: what we think, thoughts and evaluations.

Company strategy: more than a signal of quality; it's a way to communicate intangibles, for example, passion or excitement.

Design experience: goes beyond usability and requires treating the user holistically as a feeling, thinking, active person.

Digital affect: what is evoked when a customer consumes, interacts or has contact with a company's digital stimulus.

Digital Affect Framework: the overarching theoretical framework constructed and presented in the book.

Digital channel: a collective term to describe technology-based platforms that use the internet to connect with customers, provide a range of different content and purposes, and facilitate communication with a range of different levels of interaction.

Digital hedonic rhetoric: the outcome of **affective state classification**. It is used to identify the affect of a company's value proposition to inform the selection of the digital stimulus. It is also used to understanding what affective state you aim to evoke when a customer engages with the digital stimulus.

Digital platforms: another term for digital channels.

Digital relationships: the process of creating a connection between a company and a customer through digital channels. This relationship provides the benefits of connectivity and convenience, however it requires an understanding of customer needs.

Digital stimulus: a collective term to describe technology-based platforms.

Digital strategy: an alignment of a company's business strategy and information technology to gain a competitive advantage.

Digital touchpoint: the individual digital channel (e.g. website or a mobile application).

Digital typology: the grouping of digital touchpoints with common meta-characteristics, such as the content displayed, the purpose, the direction of communication and the interaction rank. There are four digital typologies: functional, social, community and corporate.

Emotions: brief, but often intense, mental and physiological feeling states. In comparison with moods, emotions are shorter lived, stronger, and more specific forms of affect.

Emotional affect: is defined by Donald Norman as

> the general term for the judgmental system, whether conscious or unconscious. Emotion is the conscious experience of affect complete with attribution of its cause and identification of its object. A queasy, uneasy feeling you might experience, without knowing why, is affect.[7]

Emotional design: a field of research dealing with how a designer elicits emotions through the manipulation of a product's sensory qualities. The concept of experience, where the subject and object meet and merge, becomes in turn a key issue in designing emotionally meaningful products. Donald Norman defined this field in 2004.

Emotional engagement: develops when a customer identifies with the values and behaviours of a company.

Emotion process: modelled from Damasio's somatic feedback theory,[6] a typical case begins with perceptions about a stimulus (A), leading to thoughts and evaluations about the stimulus (B), this mental activity triggers a bodily reaction (C) to create a certain activity in the body (D).

Feelings: subjective representations of emotions, private to the individual experiencing them. Rosalind Picard defines 'feelings' strictly as a physical sensory input, however is aware that they are sometimes equal with emotional experience. There are different types of feelings, depending on the way they are triggered, either internal (physical) feelings or external (social) feelings. Feelings evoke emotions.

Hedonics: the pursuit of pleasure, and in this book, the examination of how an individual actively pursues pleasure by responding to certain objects and experiences.

Mood: a long-term affective state that is triggered by a combination of emotions. Moods are diffused affective states that generally last for a much longer duration and are usually less intense than emotions.

Receiver: the customer who receives the message from the source.

Source: the creator of the message (what should be communicated to customers).

Transmitter: the digital stimulus, which transmits the message from the source to the receiver.

Value proposition: a company's current business purpose, a promise of value to be delivered, communicated and experienced by the customer. A value proposition, as a statement, clearly identifies what benefits a customer will receive by purchasing a particular product or service from a vendor.

Personal reflections and acknowledgements

It is no secret that business in Australia has been affected by an influx of international competition. The companies we have worked with to date are feeling this pressure immensely and looking to design innovation for a competitive advantage to remain relevant in the future. These (small to medium) enterprises are the backbone of our sovereign nation. Companies passed down from one generation to another are the key to driving the national competitive agenda forward in the future.

These businesses (thinking they are doing the right thing) employ well-educated people, qualified with traditional degrees from high-quality tertiary institutions such as the one we work at. There are many more graduates now seeking employment from these traditional degrees than ever before in history. As we ourselves are entrenched in education, we see students select conservative degrees in an age of constant digital disruption. The time to be bold and do things differently is upon us. The more pressing global challenges to come in the future will demand different leadership styles. The first step is awareness by the people making these decisions, and this book is only the beginning.

* * *

Many Foxes and Hedgehogs were invaluable in making this book a reality. Despite only having a decade of experience, we as authors have learnt so much from our traditional design footholds — to become the hybrids we are today.

To the plethora of colleagues and companies that have provided input, we owe special thanks.

There are so many of you to thank. We are deeply grateful in particular to: Dr Rebecca Price, who is responsible for the success that was the Brisbane Airport case study; to Dr Erez Nusem, for the spectacular illustrations throughout this book; thanks to Associate Professor Martin Tomitsch and team at the Design Lab — your support has been a welcomed change. Cj Hendry — for the wonderful front cover design and everything over the years! You are one Foxy lady!

To end on a personal note:

From Prof. C: To the few close to me — you are more than I deserve.

From Dr K: Dedicated to the original Fox — my mother — Angelika Straker.

From us both — thank you to The Sydney School of Architecture, Design and Planning for believing in us and taking a chance on two Foxes who never quit!

References

Apple.com, 2006. 'Apple Store Fifth Avenue'. Apple press release. Available at: http://www.apple.com/au/pr/library/2006/.

Apple.com, 2015b. 'Apple Brings Innovation Back to Television with The All-New Apple TV'. Press release.

Berlin, I., 1954. *The Hedgehog and the Fox*. Weidenfeld & Nicolson.

Block, R., 2007. 'Live from Macworld 2007: Steve Jobs keynote'. engadget .com. Available at: http://www.engadget.com/2007/01/09/live-from-macworld-2007-steve-jobs-keynote/.

Brien, M., 2013. 'Samsung versus Apple: Dueling business models'. Available at: http://www.domicity.com/2013/04/samsung-versus-apple/.

Brown, T., & Katz, B., 2011. 'Change by design'. *Journal of Product Innovation Management*, 28(3), pp. 381–383.

Brown, T., 2008. 'Design thinking'. *Harvard Business Review*, 86(6), pp. 84–92, 141.

Burberry.com, 2014. 'Kate Moss and Cara Delevingne shot together for the first time for new iconic fragrance — My Burberry'. Press release, available at: www.burberryplc.com/media_centre/press_releases/2014/my-burberry.

Burberry.com, 2015. 'Our strategy'. Available at: www.burberryplc.com/about_burberry/our_strategy?WT.ac1/4Our+strategy.

Collins, J. C., 2001. *Good to great: Why some companies make the leap... and others don't*. Random House.

Damasio, A. R., 2006. *Descartes' error*. Random House.

Darwin, C., 1872. *The expression of the emotions in man and animals*. John Murray.

Desmet, P., 2002. *Designing emotions*. Delft University of Technology. Department of Industrial Design.

Desmet, P., 2003. 'A multi-layered model of product emotions'. *The design journal*, 6(2), pp. 4–13.

Desmet, P., 2005. 'Measuring emotion: Development and application of an instrument to measure emotional responses to products'. In *Funology* pp. 111–123. Kluwer Academic Publishers.

Ekman, P., & Friesen, W. V., 1971. 'Constants across cultures in the face and emotion'. *Journal of personality and social psychology*, 17(2), p. 124.

Forlizzi, J., & Ford, S., 2000, August. 'The building blocks of experience: an early framework for interaction designers'. In *Proceedings of the 3rd conference on Designing interactive systems: processes, practices, methods, and techniques*, pp. 419–423. ACM.

Interbrand.com, 2013. 'Interbrand Best Brand Report 2013'. Available at: http://www.bestglobalbrands.com/previous-years/2013.

Interbrand.com, 2014. 'Interbrand Best Brand Report 2014'. Available at: http://www.bestglobalbrands.com/previous-years/2014.

International Institute for Management Development (IMD), 2017. Report available at: https://www.imd.org.

Keeley, L., Walters, H., Pikkel, R., & Quinn, B., 2013. *Ten types of innovation: The discipline of building breakthroughs*. John Wiley & Sons.

Lindström, M., 2010. *Buyology: Truth and lies about why we buy*. Crown Business.

Morris, L., 2009. 'Business model innovation the strategy of business breakthroughs'. *International Journal of Innovation Science*, 1(4), pp. 191–204.

Norman, D. A., 2004. *Emotional design: Why we love (or hate) everyday things*. Basic Civitas Books.

Picard, R. W., & Picard, R., 1997. *Affective computing*, Vol. 252. MIT Press.

Pine, B. J., & Gilmore, J. H., 1999. *The experience economy: Work is theatre & every business a stage*. Harvard Business Press.

Plutchik, R., 1980. 'A general psychoevolutionary theory of emotion'. *Theories of emotion*, 1 pp. 3–31.

Price, R. & Wrigley, C., 2016. 'Design and a deep customer insight approach to innovation'. *Journal of International Consumer Marketing*, 28(2), pp. 92–105.

Rangel, A., Camerer, C., & Montague, P. R., 2008. 'A framework for studying the neurobiology of value-based decision making'. *Nature reviews. Neuroscience*, 9(7), pp. 545–556.

Shannon, C., 1948. 'A mathematical theory of communication'. *Bell System Technical Journal*, 27, pp. 379–423.

Simon, H., 1968. *The sciences of the artificial*. Cambridge: M.I.T. Press.

Straker, K., & Wrigley, C., 2018. 'Engaging passengers across digital channels: An international study of 100 airports.' *Journal of Hospitality and Tourism Management*. 34, pp. 82–92

Straker, K. & Wrigley, C., 2016. 'Translating emotional insights into digital channel designs: Opportunities to enhance the airport experience'. *Journal of Hospitality and Tourism Technology*, 7(2), pp. 135–157.

Straker, K., & Wrigley, C., 2016. 'Designing an emotional strategy: Strengthening digital channel engagements'. *Business Horizons*, 59(3), pp. 339–346.

Straker, K., & Wrigley, C., 2016. 'Emotionally engaging customers in the digital age: The case study of "Burberry love"'. *Journal of Fashion Marketing and Management*, 20(3), pp. 276–299.

Straker, K., & Wrigley, C., 2016. 'The role of emotion, experience and meaning: The comparative case of Apple and Samsung'. In *International perspectives on business innovation and disruption in design*, pp. 231–255. Edward Elgar Publishing Limited.

Straker, K., Wrigley, C., & Rosemann, M., 2015. 'The role of design in the future of digital channels: Conceptual insights and future research directions'. *Journal of Retailing and Consumer Services*, 26, pp. 133–140.

Straker, K., Wrigley, C., & Rosemann, M., 2015. 'Typologies and touchpoints: Designing multi-channel digital strategies'. *Journal of Research in Interactive Marketing*, 9(2), pp. 110–128.

Vygotsky, L. S., 1980. *Mind in society: The development of higher psychological processes*. Harvard University Press.

Wrigley, C., 2013. 'Design dialogue: The visceral hedonic rhetoric framework'. *Design Issues*, 29(2), pp. 82–95.

Wrigley, C., & Straker, K., 2016. 'Designing innovative business models with a framework that promotes experimentation'. *Strategy & Leadership*, 44(1), pp. 11–19.

Young, P. T., 1961. *Motivation and emotion: A survey of the determinants of human and animal activity*. Oxford, England.

Endnotes

1. Desmet, P., 2002. *Designing emotions*. Delft University of Technology. Department of Industrial Design.

2. Pine, B. J., & Gilmore, J. H., 1999. The experience economy: Work is theatre & every business a stage. Harvard Business Press.

3. Damasio, A., 1994. *Descartes' error: Emotion, reason, and the human brain*. Putnam.

4. ibid., p. 155.

5. Desmet, P., 2005. 'Measuring emotion: Development and application of an instrument to measure emotional responses to products'. In *Funology*, pp. 111–123. Kluwer Academic Publishers.

6. Damasio. *Descartes' error*.

7. Norman, D. A., 2004. *Emotional design: Why we love (or hate) everyday things*. Basic Civitas Books, p. 11.

Index